W9-AAH-027

Collecting Child Support

Susan Herskowitz, Esq

Made E-Z

An Official
Made E-Z Product

MADE E-Z PRODUCTS™ Inc.
Deerfield Beach, Florida / www.MadeE-Z.com

AUG 0 6 20??

NOTICE:

THIS PRODUCT IS NOT INTENDED TO PROVIDE LEGAL ADVICE. IT CONTAINS GENERAL INFORMATION FOR EDUCATIONAL PURPOSES ONLY. PLEASE CONSULT AN ATTORNEY IN ALL LEGAL MATTERS. THIS PRODUCT WAS NOT NECESSARILY PREPARED BY A PERSON LICENSED TO PRACTICE LAW IN YOUR STATE.

Collecting Child Support Made E-Z™
Suzan Herskowitz, Esq.

Important Notice

This product is intended for informational use only and is not a substitute for legal advice. State laws vary and change and the information or forms do not necessarily conform to the laws or requirements of your state. While you always have the right to prepare your own documents and to act as your own attorney, do consult an attorney on all important legal matters. You will find a listing of state bar referral services in the Resources section of this product. This product was not necessarily prepared by a person licensed to practice law in your state.

Table of contents

How to use this guide

The Made E-Z™ guides can help you achieve an important legal objective conveniently, efficiently and economically. But it is important to properly use this guide if you are to avoid later difficulties.

◆ Carefully read all information, warnings and disclaimers concerning the legal forms in this guide. If after thorough examination you decide that you have circumstances that are not covered by the forms in this guide, or you do not feel confident about preparing your own documents, consult an attorney.

◆ Complete each blank on each legal form. Do not skip over inapplicable blanks or lines intended to be completed. If the blank is inapplicable, mark "N/A" or "None" or use a dash. This shows you have not overlooked the item.

◆ Always use pen or type on legal documents—never use pencil.

◆ Avoid erasures and "cross-outs" on final documents. Use photocopies of each document as worksheets, or as final copies. All documents submitted to the court must be printed on one side only.

◆ Correspondence forms may be reproduced on your own letterhead if you prefer.

◆ Whenever legal documents are to be executed by a partnership or corporation, the signatory should designate his or her title.

◆ It is important to remember that on legal contracts or agreements between parties all terms and conditions must be clearly stated. Provisions may not be enforceable unless in writing. All parties to the agreement should receive a copy.

◆ Instructions contained in this guide are for your benefit and protection, so follow them closely.

◆ You will find a glossary of useful terms at the end of this guide. Refer to this glossary if you encounter unfamiliar terms.

◆ Always keep legal documents in a safe place and in a location known to your spouse, family, personal representative or attorney.

Introduction to Collecting Child Support Made E-Z™

Raising children is an enormous financial responsibility for two parents. For one parent, it is often impossible. Every day in America more women and children enter the poverty ranks, as one of every two marriages continues to end in divorce. But why should the children suffer when that occurs?

Because all parents are legally obligated to support their children financially, many states have enacted laws making it a crime for non-custodial parents to neglect child support payments. Some states, particularly Florida, jail deadbeat parents who fail to make timely support payments. And in 1992, the federal government made it a crime for a parent to evade support payments for a child living in another state.

You may be one of the lucky ones whose ex-spouse regularly makes monthly or annual support payments, exercises visitation rights, and takes an active interest in your children. But what if that changes? Are you prepared to take the necessary steps to guarantee your children continue to get paid? What if your child's needs change? Do you know how or when to petition the court for a modification of the award?

You should learn about the child support collection process if you find yourself in any of the following situations:

- your ex-spouse currently pays child support but owes back support
- your ex-spouse sporadically pays child support and now owes back support
- your ex-spouse is not paying any child support, and there is a delinquency
- your ex-spouse owes back support and is nowhere to be found

Even if you currently receive payments and have never experienced delinquencies, circumstances often change, and it would benefit you to learn about the child support collection process. Of course, the best way to guarantee prompt child support payments is for you to maintain a working relationship with your ex-spouse. This will greatly benefit your children because when parents communicate and cooperate with each other, an ex-spouse will usually exercise visitation rights. And, when your ex-spouse visits, that usually encourages more regular support payments.

This guide discusses the steps you can take to collect the child support due you and offers other options available to you if your child support has not been paid.

Note: Although parentage does not always involve marriage, throughout this guide the term ex-spouse refers to the non-custodial parent (the parent who does not have custody of the child).

Parents' rights and obligations

1

Chapter 1

Parents' rights and obligations

What you'll find in this chapter:

➤ Making custody decisions

➤ Establishing visitation rights

➤ A parent's legal obligations

➤ Child support issues

➤ What a court considers

Anyone facing divorce or separation is faced with a million personal issues, be they emotional, physical, or financial. Any parent facing divorce or separation, however, has an even greater set of issues to deal with: their children. First, who will get custody of the children? Second, what kind of visitation will the non-custodial parent be granted? Third, how much child support will the non-custodial parent be obligated to pay?

Custody

The most emotional part of a divorce or separation involves the custody decision. It is also the most important. If you have children, the court will compel you and your ex-spouse to maintain as harmonious a relationship as possible, because your cooperation is vital to the well-being of your children.

In the past there was a strong presumption that the mother would make the best custodial parent. This is because the mother was the homemaker and caretaker of the children, while the husband was the breadwinner. This presumption was particularly true with younger children and daughters.

Fathers, in the past, could only hope for custody by convincing the court that the mother was unfit to care for the children. This usually meant that the mother was an alcoholic, on drugs or otherwise unsuitable because of psychological or behavioral problems that would be injurious to the children.

> *note*
>
> In more recent years the presumption that the mother is the best custodian of the children has weakened.

Courts now consider what's in the best interests of the children when deciding upon the custodial parent. As a practical matter this still ends up being the mother in the vast majority of cases.

DEFINITION

Before we proceed further it is important to understand the different types of custody. Historically, *sole custody* was the usual form of custody. That meant that the custodial parent had both *physical custody* or possession of the child and *legal custody* or sole authority to make all decisions concerning the child. This type of custody, with the non-custodial parent only having visitation rights, remains the most common arrangement.

DEFINITION

In recent years the concept of *shared* or *joint custody* has gained in popularity. This means that both parents have an equal say in the upbringing of the child, that is, they share *legal custody*. One spouse may continue to have sole physical custody.

DEFINITION

Joint physical custody of the children can also be provided for. Under this type of custody, each parent has exclusive physical custody for alternating periods—which may, for example, be certain days, weeks or months per year. While it seems a fair arrangement, many courts and psychologists believe this is harmful to the stability of the child, who loses his or her sense of "home." This arrangement is also called divided or alternating custody.

Another possibility is split custody. Here each parent receives sole custody of at least one child with visitation rights to the other children. In essence, the family becomes divided. Courts understandably frown on this because it means not only separation from one's parent but also separation from siblings.

In deciding custody, more and more courts are looking to determine which parent is the more active caregiver. That is, who does the child most rely upon for day-to-day care?

> **The courts believe continuing the primary caregiver as custodian provides the child the most stability.**

Visitation

Related to the issue of custody is the matter of visitation. The parent denied physical custody of the child has the right to reasonable visitation with the children. The only exception is if the parent is abusive or behaves in a way that can be harmful to the child.

The frequency and duration of your visitation is one major decision that must be carefully worked out with your spouse. The more frequent the visits, the closer is the relationship between child and non-custodial parent. Therefore, the most liberal and flexible visitation arrangement that is possible is encouraged.

While you and your spouse may agree on custody and visitation, this is always subject to review and modification by the court. What factors will the court consider when evaluating whether your agreement is in the best interests of your children?

- the age, sex and health of the child

- the physical capability and mental willingness of each parent to provide the child's needs on a day-to-day basis

- the bond between the child and each parent

- the desires of the child (if of sufficient age and capacity)

- the desires of the parents

- the health and age of the parents

- the effect on the child of moving

Additionally, the court will more willingly grant joint custody when:

- the parents can cooperate and harmoniously make decisions together

- the relationship between the child and each parent is reasonably balanced

- both parents enthusiastically welcome joint custody

note

When considering the terms of visitation, the court will generally favor a fixed or detailed visitation schedule rather than rely on vague terms such as "reasonable visitation," which can only invite disagreement when the spouses are not getting along. You can, however, build some flexibility into your agreement as long as you stay close to the standard of what a court may consider reasonable.

A parent's legal obligations

A parent is expected to care for the well-being of his or her children, to nurture them and to love them. All parents are also legally obligated to support their children financially. When the children's parents are married to each other, this obligation is a given. It is understood that the money earned by both mother and father will be used to support the family unit. When the parents separate, divorce or never marry, however, the rules change. Often the non-custodial parent must be coerced and ordered by the court to financially support the offspring.

A parent's legal obligation to support his or her children financially exists until:

- the children reach adulthood, usually age 18, although if the child is disabled, the obligation may be extended. In fact, a court may order that support for a disabled child be continued indefinitely.

- the children begin active military duty

- the children are emancipated by a court of law, which means that the children, although they are not yet 18 years of age, are considered adults by law

- the children, still under the age of 18, get married

- the parents' rights and responsibilities are terminated by law. This must be accomplished by a formal court hearing and usually occurs when a child is being adopted. The natural parents' rights must be extinguished before another person may adopt the child.

In general, death of the non-custodial parent ends the obligation to support the children.

The custodial parent, in addition to the everyday responsibilities of being an only parent, often finds himself or herself scrounging for enough money to keep the children housed, clothed and fed.

note Unfortunately, the majority of custodial parents in this country receive only occasional monetary help from non-custodial parents, if any help at all.

That is where the courts step in. Custodial parents may be awarded child support that is a legally enforceable obligation of the non-custodial parent. A custodial parent can also turn to the court to modify the amount of support and ensure the payment of support, even across state lines. But first, we will take a look at how custodial parents can be awarded the child support they need.

Child support

The obligation of the parent to support a child is basic and one strongly enforced by the courts. Most judges look closest at this issue realizing it is here where the agreement may be inequitable and not adequately provide for the minor child.

> **note** The goal is to provide the children with as much support as possible and at the same time leave the obligated parent with sufficient income to live in reasonable style. Achieving these two objectives is seldom easy.

Some states have guidelines for support. Often, the obligated spouse (usually the husband) believes he does not have sufficient income to adequately support both himself and his children.

What does a court consider in awarding support?

- the number of children and their ages. Courts may award less support when you have teenage children with some earning power of their own.

- whether the custodial spouse has any earning capabilities and can contribute to the support of the children

- the health or special needs of the children

- the income of the obligated spouse, as well as the earnings potential

- the assets or wealth of the obligated spouse

- other financial responsibilities of the obligated spouse, including support obligations from a prior marriage

> **note** Child support, like custody and visitation, is never permanent.

Either party can seek modification of the terms for good cause. For example, the husband may lose his job or become ill—events that may, at least temporarily, justify a reduction in support. Conversely, the husband may become wealthy, prompting the ex-wife to have the court increase the support payments.

In addition to support, a parent may become obligated to provide for the child's medical care (including maintenance of health insurance) and for the child's day care costs or college education. Support may continue until the child is 18 or "emancipated"— which means that he or she is self-supporting. This is typically when the

> **HINT** For tax purposes, child support payments are not deductible as an expense, or considered income to the receiving spouse; but, alimony is tax deductible to the obligor and counted as income to the recipient.

child leaves college, and may thus extend the support obligation until the child is about 22 years old.

Obtaining an order for child support

2

Chapter 2

Obtaining an order for child support

To receive support by administrative order, you need to file a uniform petition for support (see the sample form in chapter 8). Then you need to obtain jurisdiction over your ex-spouse by applying to the appropriate agency and serving him or her with notice of the action.

Serving notice

Serving notice is a fancy way of saying you need to let somebody know about a legal action being taken, in this case that you have filed for child support. You may serve by personal service (a sheriff or private process server delivers the notice), by certified mail, and, in some states, by first-class mail return receipt requested, or by publication of the notice in a newspaper of general circulation.

The notice must contain:

- names of the children for whom you are seeking support

- rights of the non-custodial parent, including the right to a hearing and representation by counsel

- a warning that a default order may be entered if the notice is ignored

- a specific time limit for the non-custodial parent to respond

- information on the right to appeal

- the amount of current support due or any back support due under an existing order if there is one

- instructions concerning arranging a negotiation conference

- a list of collection actions that may be used to obtain the support once an administrative order is entered

Your ex-spouse may respond in one of four ways:

1) fail to take any action within the time specified

This is a default and the agency may enter an administrative order for the amount asked for in the notice.

2) consent to pay the amount asked for in the notice

3) request a negotiation conference with the agency

The non-custodial parent will likely argue for a different support amount. If an amount is agreed to, a consent order will be entered.

4) file a formal request for a hearing

A hearing will be held before an administrative hearing officer, who may be an attorney. The support enforcement hearing officer is generally given many powers and duties, including the ability to:

• issue process

• administer oaths

• require the production of documents

• conduct hearings for the purpose of taking evidence

After the request for hearing has been filed, the support enforcement hearing officer may give notice to each of the parties, assigning a time and place for an appropriate hearing as is required by state law.

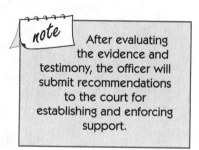

note After evaluating the evidence and testimony, the officer will submit recommendations to the court for establishing and enforcing support.

Determining child support

Under the Child Support Enforcement Act of 1984, each state must develop guidelines to calculate the amount of child support to be paid based on both parents' incomes and expenses.

States consider the following three factors when determining the amount of child support to be awarded:

1) Needs of the child, including:

• health care requirements

- day care needs

- educational needs

- special needs

2) Parent's ability to pay

3) Both parents' ability to earn

HOT spot To arrive at a parent's ability to pay, the court uses the basic formula of gross income less customary deductions to determine the parent's net income. You can use the same formula to establish for yourself a reasonable amount of child support to seek.

Using these criteria, the state strives to maintain the child's pre-divorce or pre-separation standard of living. If a child is handicapped, for example, special equipment, medication, therapy or other special requirements are taken into consideration.

Gross income includes the following:

- wages

- interest and dividends on investments

- commissions, tips and bonuses

- rental income

- service pay

- pensions

- trust income

- annuities

- capital gains

- royalties on patents or copyrights

- profits from business ventures

- self-employment income

- Social Security benefits

- unemployment benefits

- gifts and prizes

- disability and workers' compensation benefits

The mandatory deductions a court will consider include the following:

- Social Security taxes

- federal and state income tax withholding

- mandatory union dues

- health insurance expenses

Some states limit the deduction for health insurance to those payments made on behalf of the children only. Any deduction a parent may take that is not on the state's list of authorized deductions is exempt from consideration.

note The court will look at your ex-spouse's net disposable or discretionary income to determine how much is available for support before taking expenses into consideration.

However, courts also consider a parent's ability to earn when he or she leaves employment to return to school or takes a lower paying job. On occasion, a non-custodial parent will take or threaten to take a significantly lower paying job to skew the income picture just to spite the custodial parent.

 Remember: An award that is set too high will invariably result in back support; setting the award too low will undoubtedly be difficult for you and deprive your children of much needed financial support. Sometimes it is best to go for a moderate child support award, one high enough to meet the children's needs, but low enough not to overburden your ex-spouse.

Modifying your child support

Chapter 3

Modifying your child support

What you'll find in this chapter:

➡ Changes which modify support

➡ Determining the ex-'s assets

➡ Tools to gather information

➡ How to prove the need for change

➡ A reduction can occur

Once you've been awarded child support, you may find that the amount is not sufficient due to a change in your (or your ex-spouse's) financial situation. One of several things may have happened since the support was awarded:

- your income has decreased

- your child (ren)'s needs have increased

- your ex-spouse's income/assets have increased

- your ex-spouse now has less money

The court allows you to request a change in the amount of child support you receive based upon changes in your needs, your income, and your ex-spouse's income. This is done by petitioning for a modification of child support.

Determining your ex-spouse's assets

Identification of the non-custodial parent's assets will help you, your attorney or the child support enforcement agency determine if the support award should be higher than what was initially believed adequate.

The following tools may be used to identify additional assets:

- state employment agencies

- state earnings records

- credit bureaus

- banks

- motor vehicle department

Many states require employers to provide statements of an employee's earnings (usually for unemployment compensation purposes). Bank records, on the other hand, may require a subpoena. Motor vehicle records may help you discover that your ex-spouse traded in his Yugo for a Rolls Royce and probably can afford to pay more support.

All enforceable modifications must be approved by a judge. In general, you will have to prove a substantial change in circumstances. Some states will not modify the order if it has been less than two years since the order was signed and there is no evidence of hardship beyond a change in circumstances. Any of the following may convince a judge to award more support:

note When you modify an order for child support, you are asking the judge to increase the support obligation.

1) cost of living increase

2) increase in the non-custodial parent's income due to a change in job

3) medical emergencies

4) changes in your child's needs due to health or educational changes

5) additional financial expenditures

6) additional household income from the non-custodial parent's remarriage. Courts will reason that a non-custodial parent's disposable income increases upon remarriage, giving rise to justifying increased support.

7) changes in the law

On occasion, the guidelines themselves allow for an increase in support even if income and circumstances do not change. See Appendix IV for a state-by-state look at the criteria used to determine the modification of child support orders.

 Keep in mind that, just as the court may increase support based on a change in circumstances, support can be lowered as well. Your ex-spouse may petition the court to reduce the support obligation, arguing that substantial changes in circumstance—such as a loss of job or pay, or bills for medical emergencies—warrant a reduction. Make sure you have enough evidence to show that no decrease is justified.

When child support is in arrears

Chapter 4

When child support is in arrears

What you'll find in this chapter:

- ▶ Enforcing a support order
- ▶ Using public and private agencies
- ▶ Garnishment of wages
- ▶ Attaching wages
- ▶ Alternative collection methods

When you have a child support order but your ex-spouse owes some back support, the least confrontational method of collection is to ask your ex-spouse to pay the arrearage. This method will only succeed, however, if the two of you have a good working relationship.

If that method is not possible, or if you tried it and the arrearage (or overdue debt) was still not paid, you have several options to choose from in order to collect the money due you.

Enforcement by state child support agency

Every state child support agency is mandated by the federal government, under the authority of Title IV-D of the Social Security Act, to enforce child support orders for children on public assistance. No application is required and the office must assist you.

Anyone who is on welfare, or other forms of public assistance, can seek help from a state child support agency.

If you are not on public assistance, the agency can still help you, but you will be required to fill out an application. State child support enforcement agencies are listed in Appendix II, and these agencies also can provide telephone numbers for local offices. Call your local child support enforcement office to learn how to apply for enforcement services and what documents (birth certificates, financial statements, separation and/or divorce papers) you should provide when you keep your appointment.

Private enforcement agencies

Your state may allow you to hire the services of a private child support collection agency. Most agencies of this type take a percentage of the amount collected on your behalf as payment for services. These agencies often use national databases and automated dialing systems to locate and then contact child support violators. What can take the state months may take as little as two minutes for a private agency with access to these computer databases.

note If your state is using private enforcement agencies, you are indeed lucky because the cost to you will be either free or minimal, and you will have the backing of both the child support office and the private collection agency in the effort to collect the money owed your children.

Some states, mindful that they do not have the staff to be as effective as necessary, are themselves hiring private collection agencies to assist in finding absent parents and enforce support obligations. The funding to pay these agencies generally comes from federal funds provided to the state for child support enforcement purposes.

Garnishment

Garnishment entails attaching the non-custodial parent's money, including bank accounts, trust accounts, judgments, and insurance payoffs. However, your ex-spouse must have the money available to garnish. For example, if you know that your ex-spouse is about to collect a large sum of money from an insurance settlement, you may begin garnishment proceedings so you will collect any back support due up front, before your ex-spouse receives payment.

 However, note that the garnishee is not your ex-spouse but the person or company in possession of the money, such as a bank. Also note that garnishment is not the same as automatic wage withholding, which is discussed later in this guide.

How to garnish an ex-spouse's money for back support:

1) If money is available, file a motion for garnishment in your local county court.

2) In addition to a filing fee, you must fill out a form instructing the sheriff to serve the garnishee and pay a fee for service of process to the clerk. The clerk then has the county sheriff's office serve the garnishee with a copy of a writ of garnishment.

3) When the sheriff shows that the garnishee was served, the sheriff will then serve the writ and a notice of garnishment on your ex-spouse. This will produce either an order releasing your ex-spouse's money to you or an order stating that the funds will remain with the ex-spouse.

4) The ex-spouse has a time limit in which to respond and contest the garnishment. If the notice goes unanswered, you file an application to execute (levy) on the funds and have the order processed. In

almost all states, a judge must sign the order to condemn the funds.

5) Once the order is signed, the garnishee will be required to release the funds to you.

> **HOT spot** It is important to get at lump sums of money while they are available.

You may get faster results by hiring a private process server if your state allows. If you hire a private process server, you will not pay a service of process fee to the county clerk, but the fee is likely to be higher than that charged by the county.

Wage attachment

An order for wage attachment is a court order instructing your ex-spouse's employer to deduct a set amount of money from your ex-spouse's paycheck each pay period. This money is usually sent directly to the child support enforcement office, a court registry, or your state attorney general's office, which then forwards the money to you. The employer also may be required to send the money directly to you. An attachment can be used to pay past due support or to secure both current and future payments.

 Definition:

Federal law mandates that all states have some form of wage attachment, also called *automatic wage withholding.*

In some states, the non-custodial parent is automatically set up for wage attachment regardless of prior payment history. Your state may allow you to initiate wage withholding without a court order or service of process. Other states will require you to petition the court that awarded the support initially and obtain an order signed by the judge. Automatic withholding orders may take precedence over any other garnishment, attachment, execution, or other assignment or order affecting the non-custodial parent's earnings.

If the employer fails to withhold, however, he will be accountable to you.

An employer cannot be sued by your ex-spouse for attaching wages. You can recover the amounts not properly withheld from your ex-spouse's paycheck. In addition, you may be able to collect any attorney's fees and court costs incurred when suing the employer for the money.

In general, an employer may not legally discharge or discipline an employee based on the employee's child support obligations, nor may an employer refuse to hire someone because of an automatic wage withholding order. Therefore, do not allow your ex-spouse to scare you into believing that you will cause the loss of his or her job if you initiate automatic wage withholding.

Tax offset program

If you have the non-custodial parent's Social Security number, the child support office will give the number to the IRS and state revenue agencies. If your ex-spouse is entitled to a refund, it will be offset and sent to you.

note You can receive money for support due you directly from your ex-spouse's IRS tax refund.

Real estate liens

It is possible to place a lien on any real property your ex-spouse owns.

This will prevent your ex-spouse from being able to sell the property until he or she pays you. This is only a preventive measure, however, and your ex-spouse may not want to sell the property for years, so explore one of the other methods of collection as well. Some states have automatic lien laws where you do not have to file a lien; at most, you may have to file an application and the process will then proceed automatically.

Seizure and sale of property

H
I
N
T

If either you or the child support enforcement office can find property owned by your ex-spouse, you may be able to have the property seized by the county sheriff. It is then sold, and the proceeds are applied to the support arrearage. This requires you to petition the court for permission to seize the property. The sheriff will seize the property only after an order is signed by a judge. In California, however, property can be seized directly by the Franchise Tax Board.

Alternative methods

A few states have legislated new methods designed to coerce regular payments. They include:

- publishing either a complete list of the delinquent parents or only those most wanted. In some states, they are published in major newspapers and in others, names are published in poster-form complete with photographs.

- suspension or revocation of driver's license. Some states are suspending the delinquent parent's driver's license, while others are revoking the license, unless the delinquent parent contacts the support enforcement office and either pays the delinquency in full, sets up a payment plan or contests the action in court.

- statewide arrest sweeps. Delinquent parents may be arrested.

- interception of refunds. State-issued refunds are sent directly to you or the children instead of to the delinquent parent.

Recent federal laws have been introduced to make it easier to keep track of and track down delinquent parents. The Child Support Performance and Incentives Act of 1998 contains major child support enforcement provisions, including that all drivers' licenses will have Social Security numbers by October 1, 2000.

The Personal Responsibility and Work Opportunity Reconciliation Act of 1996 (PRWORA) requires employers to report certain information on their newly-hired employees to a designated state agency. After the information is reported, the states match the information against child support records to locate parents, establish an order, or enforce an existing order. Once these matches are done, the state transmits the reports to the National Directory of New Hires.

This information is not considered burdensome to employers, since the majority of the information is being reported on the employee's W-4 form. Each report must contain the employee's name, address, and Social Security number, and the employer's name, address, and Federal Employer Identification number.

Full IRS collection

To take advantage of this remedy, you must apply for state child support services. If you are a non-public assistance client, the state may require you to pay for at least part of the cost of implementing this procedure, which is a request for the U.S. Secretary of the Treasury to levy on assets.

The following information will be required by the federal government:

1) the parent's name, Social Security number, address and/or place of employment

2) copies of all court and administrative orders

3) amount of money owed under those orders

4) a statement that either you or the state has made a reasonable effort to collect the money owed

5) a description of all actions taken in an effort to collect the back support

6) dates of prior requests for referral to the Secretary of the Treasury, if any

7) a statement that the state child support enforcement agency has reason to believe that the parent has assets the Secretary of the Treasury might levy

8) a statement of the nature and location of the assets

The IRS then attempts to collect the back support as if it was collecting a tax delinquency. It will not, however, charge interest or penalty on the amount owed. Due to a 60-day stay on the collection (meaning nothing will be done for 60 days), the non-custodial parent has a chance to either pay the back support or contest it.

The self-employed ex-spouse

A self-employed non-custodial parent poses a dilemma for the custodial parent. Unless your ex-spouse runs a corporation that pays a set salary, automatic wage withholding is not an option since there is no identifiable salary.

It is important to determine what assets your ex-spouse has. You may have to seize both personal and business assets. Once you find out where the money is, follow the procedures for garnishment and obtain an order to condemn the assets.

In what type of business is your ex-spouse involved?

- **Sole proprietorship**. This is the easiest type of business from which to seize assets because all assets are owned directly by the business owner. You may be able to get a levy on cash register receipts, bank accounts and receivables.

- **Partnership.** Your ex-spouse's interest in the partnership may have to be assessed and liquidated. The other partner(s) must then, following the provisions of the partnership agreement, either sell off the assets and give each partner his fair share, allow a third party to buy into the partnership, or buy out your ex-spouse and pay you the proceeds. This may force the partnership into bankruptcy. If this case applies to you, consult an attorney.

- **Corporation.** This is another type of business for which using the services of a lawyer is recommended. Methods of collection from a corporation include:

  - garnishment, in which the corporation itself is the garnishee.

  - a turnover, which directs the non-custodial parent to give you his or her share of stock certificates, which are evidence of ownership in the corporation.

HINT: At most, you may be able to seize the shares your ex-spouse owned and sell them for their current value.

If the corporation was wholly owned by your ex-spouse, you can then have the assets sold in a sheriff's sale. If it is a large, widely-held corporation, however, selling the assets can be problematic.

The unemployed ex-spouse

When your ex-spouse is unemployed, your remedies are much more limited. There are no wages to withhold and probably there will be no large sums of money to be found. The laws vary in each state, but it may be possible to attach unemployment benefits, Social Security income, workers' compensation, trust income, or retirement benefits.

HOT spot In almost all states, a parent may be prosecuted for failure to support his or her children. Because an ex-spouse in jail is unable to resume his support payments, this method is a last resort.

If all else fails, consider having your ex-spouse cited for contempt of court. This means the person is violating a legally enforceable court order. In this case, your ex-spouse is violating an order to pay child support. To avoid the contempt order, your ex-spouse will have to pay the back support or face going to jail.

When your ex-spouse lives out-of-state

5

Chapter 5

When your ex-spouse lives out-of-state

Although state enforcement agencies must cooperate with each other in handling requests for assistance, each state has an independent court system with different laws, practices and traditions. It is not simple for one state to automatically enforce the court orders of another state. But under uniform reciprocal enforcement laws, each state can refer cases to other states as well as work on cases sent to it by others.

note Laws include a provision designed to ensure that when more than one state is involved there is only one valid child support order to enforce.

Interstate wage withholding can be used to enforce a support order in another state if the non-custodial parent's employer is known. If this method is used, weeks of waiting for court dates will be unnecessary. The child support enforcement office in the state where the non-custodial parent lives will ensure that a wage withholding order from another state contains all the required information and will forward it to the non-custodial parent's employer. The order does not have to go through the courts as it would with an interstate child support enforcement petition.

 Since state laws vary, you should ask your local child support agency whether this technique is appropriate in your case.

Uniform Interstate Family Support Act

Until May of 1998, most states either followed the Uniform Reciprocal Enforcement of Support Act (URESA), or the Revised Uniform Reciprocal Enforcement of Support Act (RURESA). These acts allowed a state to collect support from another state, which was a lengthy and complicated process. The state court would contact your ex-spouse's state court, which then enforced the action on your state's behalf.

Definition:

Personal jurisdiction means that a state court or agency has the legal authority to make decisions which directly affect an individual.

Then came Uniform Interstate Family Support Act (UIFSA), which many states had adopted to replace URESA and RURESA. UIFSA bypasses the "middle man" once used with URESA and RURESA by allowing a state to proceed directly against the non-resident parent. The state can do this if it is able to assert personal jurisdiction over that non-resident under its "long-arm statute." As of May 6, 1998, UIFSA is in effect in all states.

State courts and agencies generally have personal jurisdiction over all individuals residing within their state. The most common method for a state court to assert personal jurisdiction over non-residents is through the use of long-arm jurisdiction.

The use of a long-arm statute is advantageous because it:

- removes the necessity of involving two state courts and two child support enforcement agencies

- allows for more control over the case

- permits your state to apply its own child support guidelines

- decreases the amount of time needed when documents must be transferred between two states

- eliminates the need for you and your witnesses to travel to another state for a court hearing

The circumstances supporting the assertion of specific long-arm jurisdiction should be included in any interstate order for support. This will lessen the chances of it being challenged or upheld later on. Some facts that qualify for jurisdiction in most states are that the non-resident party:

- was personally served within this state

- knowingly and voluntarily submitted to the jurisdiction of this state

- has previously resided with the child in this state

- previously resided in this state and provided prenatal expenses or support for the child

- caused the child to move to another state

- engaged in sexual intercourse in this state with the child's mother during the period in question and the child may have been conceived by that act of intercourse (used in paternity actions)

- asserted paternity in the putative (alleged) father registry filed with the appropriate agency in this state (used in paternity actions)

The standards vary, so be sure to check with your state child enforcement support agency, listed in Appendix II, for the laws specific to your state, and Appendix IV for state specific criteria for interstate procedures and jurisdiction requirements. This office reviews incoming interstate child support cases to make sure the information given is complete, sends them to the right local office, and responds to inquiries from other child support offices.

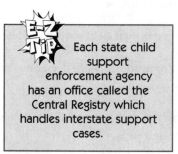

Each state child support enforcement agency has an office called the Central Registry which handles interstate support cases.

Help from the federal government

There are three provisions of the federal government that aid in collecting child support from non-custodial parents living in a different state.

The Child Support Recovery Act

The Child Support Recovery Act of 1992 made it a federal crime to willfully fail to pay support for a child living in another state. To prosecute under this act, the U.S. Attorney's Office must prove that the non-custodial parent was financially able to meet his or her obligation at the time the payment was due. If support arrearages are more than $5,000, or are unpaid for longer than one year, the non-custodial parent may be convicted of a felony.

Priority is given to cases in which the non-custodial parent displays:

- a pattern of moving from state to state to avoid payment

- a pattern of deception, such as using a false name or Social Security number

- a failure to make support payments after being held in contempt of court

- a connection between his failure to make support payments and some other federal offense, such as bankruptcy fraud

The Deadbeat Parents Punishment Act

On June 24, 1998, new legislation was signed called the Deadbeat Parents Punishment Act of 1998, which created two new categories of felonies, each with penalties of up to two years in prison:

1) A non-custodial parent who travels across state or country lines with the intent to evade child support payments may be convicted of a felony if his obligation has remained unpaid for a period longer than one year or is greater than $5,000.

2) If a non-custodial parent has traveled across state or country lines and the obligation has remained for a period of longer than two years or is greater than $10,000, his willful failure to pay child support to a child residing in another state is considered a felony.

 Since there are established procedures for referral to the U.S. Attorney's Office, and only cases that no longer can be enforced at the local level are accepted, you should always contact your local or state child support enforcement agency before pursuing federal action.

Accountability of federal employees

Master files of delinquent parents, sent by each state child support enforcement agency to the IRS, are matched at least annually to lists of federal personnel files to determine if there are any federal employees with child support delinquencies. This matched list is then forwarded to the appropriate state child enforcement agency to determine what enforcement actions should be used to collect the delinquencies. The federal government checks its personnel lists to insure accountability of its employees. This includes making all federal employees available for service of process, even if stationed outside the United States.

International remedies

If your ex-spouse is not a federal government employee and lives outside the United States, it may be more difficult to collect the support due you. There are numerous international treaties to assist you in dealing with support enforcement in foreign countries, but it is generally too difficult to accomplish without an attorney and is often necessary to hire foreign counsel. You can get information on hiring foreign counsel by writing:

> Office of Citizens' Counselor Service
> Room 4817, U.S. Department of State
> Washington, D.C. 20520

You can also contact the U.S. embassy or consulate in the foreign country.

When your ex-spouse is missing

Chapter 6

When your ex-spouse is missing

Interstate child support enforcement works well, assuming that you know where your ex-spouse lives. But what if you can't locate him or her?

Methods of location

Before you can enforce a child support order, you must find out where the missing parent lives or works. It is vital that you know your ex-spouse's full name and Social Security number. Only then can your search begin.

There are agencies set up by federal and state governments to locate absent non-custodial parents so child support obligations can be enforced. These are the same agencies that assist in locating missing children who were abducted and concealed by a parent.

Using a parent locator service

 The Federal Parent Locator Service is a nationwide tele-communications network. It links every state to the records of the IRS, Department of Defense, Social Security Administration and Veterans Administration. Ask the state-administrated child support office in your area to access the network on your behalf.

You may also get information from:

- state bureau of vital statistics

- chamber of commerce

- hospital admission records

- licensing boards

- department of motor vehicles

- local recorder's office (such as real estate recording)

- directories (such as phone books)

- relatives

- neighbors

- former employers

- friends

Private investigator or child support agency

If you cannot obtain sufficient information to begin the search or had no luck with the state locator service, you may consult a private investigator or support agency. Read your contract carefully. Also beware that many states do not require professional licensure of these agencies. Ask to see evidence of a license if your state does issue them.

Paternity

Chapter 7
Paternity

Paternity suits are initiated so a man can be declared the father of a child. Either the mother or putative (alleged) father may bring the suit. If paternity is established, the court will either grant the father custody, or order him to pay child support and

> **note** Marriage is not the controlling factor in establishing a support obligation. Parentage is.

 Definition:

Paternity actions are also called establishment hearings, filiation hearings, or parentage actions.

allow him visitation rights. Most paternity actions are initiated by welfare officials who provide Aid to Families with Dependent Children (AFDC) and are required by law to seek reimbursement from a non-custodial father.

Establishing paternity

 Even if you know who the father of your child is, you cannot expect to receive child support unless the law recognizes the father. Having the father named on the birth certificate is not, by itself, enough to enforce child support. Since 1993, upon the birth of a child to an unmarried woman in a hospital, a federally mandated hospital-based paternity program must provide to both the mother and alleged father, if present:

- written materials about establishing paternity

- forms necessary to voluntarily acknowledge paternity

- a written description of the rights and responsibilities of acknowledging paternity

- the opportunity to speak with trained staff

- the opportunity to voluntarily acknowledge paternity

- counseling about the responsibilities and obligations of acknowledging paternity

Benefits your children may obtain from establishing paternity include:

- Social Security benefits if the father dies

- Social Security benefits if the child becomes disabled while still a minor

- inheritance from the father even if not named in a will

- dependent benefits under workers' compensation laws if the father is injured at work

- military benefits, including health care, insurance or education benefits, if the father was in the service

Filing a contested paternity suit

When the alleged father is sued for paternity, he has two choices. He can admit that he is the father or deny it. Fathers typically denying paternity claim that:

- one of the parents is sterile

- the child bears no resemblance to the father

- the use of contraceptives should have prevented pregnancy

- the father had sex with the mother only once

- the mother had multiple sex partners

Often the father will deny paternity simply because he recognizes that he will be obligated to pay child support.

Genetic testing

Blood and DNA tests can affirmatively determine paternity with 99.99 percent accuracy and can show that a man is not the father with 100 percent accuracy.

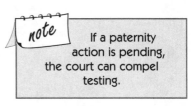

note If a paternity action is pending, the court can compel testing.

Here are three situations which may require genetic testing:

1) If the mother had multiple partners and is unsure who the child's father is, genetic testing will narrow the possibilities. The mother may name each alleged father in individual lawsuits or in one lawsuit as joint defendants.

2) If the mother and alleged father live in different states, the local child support enforcement agency can set up the appointments for blood tests on your behalf. If you are not using the state agency, you will have to contact the medical examiner in the other state for the name of a local hospital. Notify all the individuals who will be having blood drawn of the date. Give plenty of notice.

3) If paternity is uncontested, some states require the father to establish paternity legally even after he has signed a written document in which he admits paternity. Other states require testimony from both parents before legal paternity can be established. And others allow the father to sign a document stipulating paternity and consenting to entry of a judgment whereby he agrees to pay child support.

Many people believe that if the father has signed the birth certificate and lives with the mother, it is enough. If you and the father are separated, only a legal declaration of paternity can impose upon the father the legal obligation to support his children.

 Because a paternity suit is complicated, particularly if the father lives in another state, it is recommended that you consult an attorney when filing this type of legal action.

Forms you may encounter

Chapter 8

Forms you may encounter

What you'll find in this chapter:

➠ Common sections of legal forms

➠ The role of a notary

➠ Non-lawyer disclosure clause

➠ When to use an attorney

➠ Sample forms

The following chapter offers you samples of forms you will most likely encounter when you begin child support collection. Although forms vary widely from state to state, and additional forms specific to your state or area may be required, any form filed with the court generally has the same format. The samples in this chapter refer to the various steps involved in the child support collection process, and each one has a blank equivalent in the section titled, "Sample Forms in This Guide."

Common sections of legal forms

For a given legal action, there may be as many types of forms involved for that action as there are states or counties. Even forms produced by the federal government can differ—if only minutely—from city to state to region.

The forms used in collecting child support, for example, are generally state specific, so, depending on the county involved, there could be thousands of variations of the same form. In addition, every court may have its own preferred procedures for filling out and filing forms.

However, this does not mean you cannot familiarize yourself with the types of forms you may need to use or you may receive while collecting the support due you. And there are a few sections found on many types of legal forms which, aside from minor format or wording differences, have pretty much the same attributes. We will now take a look at three of the most often found sections of legal forms.

The caption

The caption is found at the top of a legal form and contains basic information regarding a court case. Legal forms that will be filed in court or recorded need to have a caption at the top. Captions always:

- identify the court by name and address

- identify the parties by name and title (contact the clerk of your local court for the specific titles used when filing in your state)

- contain a reference number called a case number

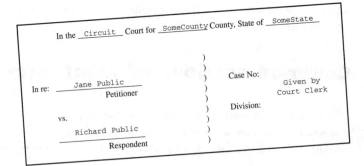

Notary clause

The notary clause is a sworn statement by the notary that he or she witnessed the signature(s) and that the person(s) signing the document is the person(s) he, she, or they claim to

If the person signing the document is not personally known to the notary, ID may be necessary.

be. All persons required to sign a notarized document must swear to their identity and sign the document while in the presence of the notary, or the document is not notarized.

STATE OF _____ SomeState _____

COUNTY OF _____ SomeCounty _____

Sworn to (or affirmed) and subscribed before me on _____ SomeDate _____, 19 96

by _____ Jane Public _____.

Witness my hand and official seal.

_____ Nick Notary _____
Signature of Notary

Affiant: _____ known _____ ✔ Produced ID

Non-lawyer disclosure clause

HOT spot

Anyone who helps you in filling out a legal form—and who is not a lawyer—is now required to fill out this clause. Courts recently began requiring the completion of this section, insisting upon full disclosure of all persons involved in the filling out of a legal form, even if you ask someone to show you where to sign your name.

IF A NONLAWYER HELPED YOU FILL OUT THIS FORM HE/SHE MUST FILL IN THE BLANKS BELOW [FILL IN ALL BLANKS]

I, (name of nonlawyer) _____ Joe Friend _____, a nonlawyer, located at

(street) 1300 SomeStreet (city) Anytown (state) SomeState 00001 ,

(phone) (123)456-7890 , helped (name) Jane Public ,

who is the (petitioner) (respondent), fill out this form.

Child support forms

The rest of this chapter will take you through the various forms you are likely to see and use in the child support collection process:

- Uniform Support Petition
- Order Requiring Payment Through Central Depository
- Motion for Health Insurance Coverage
- Non-Military Affidavit
- Financial Affidavit (Short Form)
- Summons
- Process Service Memorandum
- Motion for Garnishment After Judgment
- Final Judgment Modifying Child Support

Please keep in mind that many forms for child support must be supplied by the state and the courts, and may require more than is stated here. Contact the appropriate child support enforcement agency for forms and procedures specific to your state (Resources and Appendix I contain addresses and phone numbers for state offices; Appendix II contains regional offices).

Uniform Support Petition

This basic form outlines exactly what the custodial parent is seeking from the court. The petitioner is the one who is asking for the support and, by using a series of checkmarks, can answer the court's questions. This form often begins the legal process of obtaining child support, medical coverage, back support (arrearage), payment of court costs and attorney fees, and establishing paternity. It is signed by the custodial parent whose signature must be notarized.

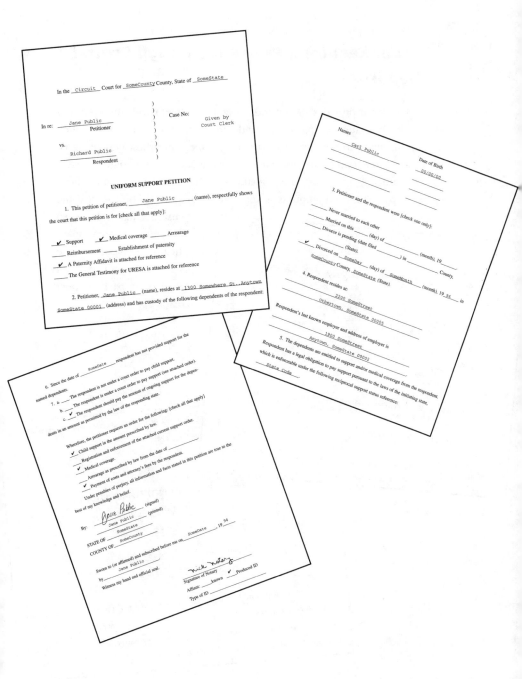

In the __Circuit__ Court for __SomeCounty__ County, State of __SomeState__

)
)
In re: __Jane Public__) Case No: Given by
_____Petitioner_____) Court Clerk
)
)
vs.)
__Richard Public__)
_____Respondent_____)

UNIFORM SUPPORT PETITION

1. This petition of petitioner, __Jane Public__ (name), respectfully shows the court that this petition is for [check all that apply]:

✓ Support   ✓ Medical coverage   _____ Arrearage
_____ Reimbursement   _____ Establishment of paternity
✓ A Paternity Affidavit is attached for reference
_____ The General Testimony for URESA is attached for reference

2. Petitioner, __Jane Public__ (name), resides at __1300 Somewhere St., Anytown SomeState 00001__ (address) and has custody of the following dependents of the respondent:

Names

__Carl Public__   Date of Birth
_____   __00/00/00__
_____
_____

3. Petitioner and the respondent were [check one only]:

_____ Never married to each other
_____ Married on this _____ (day) of
_____ Divorce is pending (date filed _____
    _____ (State).   (month), 19 ___
✓ Divorced on __SomeDay__ (day) of __SomeMonth__ (month), 19 _96_ in
__SomeCounty__ County, __SomeState__ (State).   County,

4. Respondent resides at:

__2200 SomeStreet__
__Othertown, SomeState 00005__

Respondent's last known employer and address of employer is

__1900 SomeStreet__
__Anytown, SomeState 00002__

5. The dependents are entitled to support and/or medical coverage from the respondent.
Respondent has a legal obligation to pay support pursuant to the laws of the initiating state,
which is enforceable under the following reciprocal support status reference:

__State Code__

---

6. Since the date of __SomeDate__ respondent has not provided support for the named dependents.

7. a. _____ The respondent is not under a court order to pay child support.
b. _____ The respondent is under a court order to pay support (see attached order).
c. ✓ The respondent should pay the amount of ongoing support for the dependents in an amount as permitted by the law of the responding state.

Wherefore, the petitioner requests an order for the following: [check all that apply]

✓ Child support in the amount prescribed by the attached current support order.
_____ Registration and enforcement of the attached current support order.
✓ Medical coverage.
_____ Arrearage as prescribed by law from the date of _____
✓ Payment of costs and attorney's fees by the respondent.

Under penalties of perjury, all information and facts stated in this petition are true to the best of my knowledge and belief.

By: _Jane Public_ (signed)
    __Jane Public__ (printed)

STATE OF __SomeState__
COUNTY OF __SomeCounty__

Sworn to (or affirmed) and subscribed before me on __SomeDate__, 19 _96_
by __Jane Public__
Witness my hand and official seal.

Nick Notary
Signature of Notary   ✓ Produced ID
Affiant: _____ known _____ Produced ID

Type of ID _____

Order Requiring Payment Through Central Depository

This form provides the custodial parent (obligee) with the option of having all child support payments paid directly to the court, which then transfers payment to the custodial parent. In some states the payments must be made to the child support enforcement agency or the state attorney general's office. This arrangement guarantees that an accurate and official record of payments and amounts is kept. Such a record can be useful if the non-custodial parent (obligor) is reluctant to pay, pays erratically, disputes the amount, does not pay on time, or owes back support (arrearage).

In the _Circuit_ Court for _SomeCounty_ County, State of _SomeState_

In re: ___Jane Public___
        Petitioner

vs.

___Richard Public___
        Respondent

Case No: Given by
        Court Clerk

ORDER REQUIRING PAYMENT THROUGH CENTRAL DEPOSITORY
[check all which apply and fill in all blanks that apply]

IT IS ORDERED AND ADJUDGED

that all payments of child support shall be as follows:

_____ Obligor will make the payments ordered - Fill out A & B below, NOT C.

  ✔ Payment will be by income deduction order and payor is not the obligor -

...ey will be paid and in the amount this order says will be ...mething else.

CLERK OF COURT, CENTRAL DEPOSITORY

Address _____1000 Legal Avenue_____

Anytown,   SomeState   00002
City   State   Zip

Telephone No. ___(123) 444-5555___

Telefax No. ____(123) 444-6666___

7.   Payment shall be made by cash, check, or money order. For identification and accounting purposes, you must write the court case number on each payment made by check or money order and be attached on a separate sheet of paper with any case payment. If payment is made by check, the clerk may require the payor to fill out a form.

In the ___Circuit___ Court for ___SomeCounty___ County, State of ___SomeState___

```
                                    )
                                    )     Case No:
In re:  ___Jane Public___           )           Given By
              Petitioner            )           Court Clerk
                                    )
vs.                                 )
                                    )
    ___Richard Public___            )
              Respondent            )
```

MOTION FOR HEALTH INSURANCE COVERAGE

1. On ___SomeDate___ 19 96, this court ordered the child(ren)'s

   [check one only] ✔ father or ___ mother to provide health insurance coverage for

   the following child(ren):

Name	Date Of Birth	Age	Soc. Sec. No.
Carl Public	00/00/00	6	454-45-5454

2. Notice to [check one only] ___ Petitioner or ✔ Respondent:

   [check one only]

   ✔ a. On ___SomeDate___, which is at least 15 days before filing this

application, I gave written notice of my intent to seek this order to ___Respondent___ by

[check one only] ✔ certified mail ___personal service.

___ b. The requirement of written notice has been waived by the other party.

3. I ask the court to order the employer, or other person providing health insurance coverage available to father/mother.

age to enroll or maintain the child(ren) on any health insurance coverage available to

I CERTIFY THAT THE MOTION FOR HEALTH INSURANCE COVERAGE WAS:

(check one only) ✔ mailed, ___telefaxed and mailed, or ___ hand delivered to the person(s) listed below on ___SomeDate___ ,19 96 .

Party or their attorney (if represented)

Name ___SomePerson___	Other
Address ___1111 SomeStreet___	Name
___Othertown, SomeState 00005___	Address
City State Zip	
Telephone No. ___(321) 098-7654___	City State Zip
Telefax No. ___(000) 123-4567___	Telephone No.
	Telefax No.

DATED: ___SomeDate___

Signature of party signing certificate and pleading ___Jane Public___

Printed name ___Jane Public___

Address ___1300 Somewhere Street___

City ___Anytown,___ State ___SomeState___ Zip ___00001___

Telephone (area code and number) ___(123)456-7890___

Telefax (area code and number) ___(123)456-7891___

Motion for Health Insurance Coverage

Once the court has ordered the non-custodial parent to provide health insurance coverage for the child(ren), this form asks the court to order the employer or other insurance provider (through an order for health insurance coverage) to enroll or maintain the child(ren) in any program available to the non-custodial parent.

STATE OF ___SomeState___

COUNTY OF ___SomeCounty___

Sworn to (or affirmed) and subscribed before me on ___SomeDate___, 19 96

by ___Jane Public___.

Witness my hand and official seal.

___nick notary___

Signature of Notary

Affiant: ✔ known ✔ Produced ID

Type of ID ___SomeState Driver's License___

IF A NONLAWYER HELPED YOU FILL OUT THIS FORM HE/SHE MUST FILL IN THE BLANKS BELOW [FILL IN ALL BLANKS]

I, (name of nonlawyer) ___Joe Friend___, a nonlawyer, located at (street) ___1300 SomeStreet___ (city) ___Anytown___ (state) ___SomeState, 00001___, (phone) ___(123)456-7890___, helped (name) ___Jane Public___, who is the (petitioner) (respondent), fill out this form.

Non-Military Affidavit

If either parent is in the military, professional advice should be sought. The rules and regulations allowing military personnel to participate in civil actions vary widely from state to state. Use this form when you know that neither parent is on active military service.

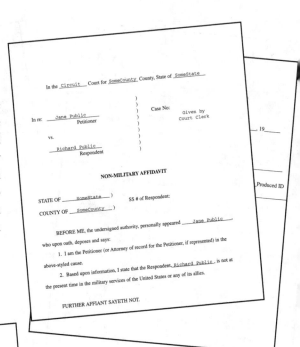

Financial Affidavit

This is an example of the kind of detailed information your state will require both parents to provide. Since every state has its own guidelines for determining the amount of child support, a financial affidavit listing current assets and liabilities allows the court to determine a reasonable amount of support.

Summons

This form is the document served upon the non-custodial parent, commanding him or her to appear in court. The manner in which it may be served varies from state to state, but typically it may be served in person, by certified mail, first-class return receipt requested, or by publication in a newspaper of general circulation. Service by publication is usually used when an ex-spouse can't be located.

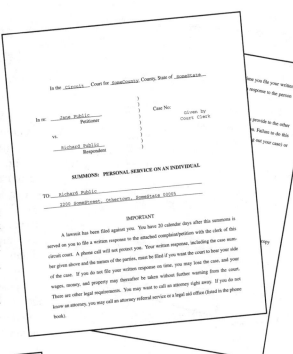

In the _Circuit_ Court for _SomeCounty_ County, State of _SomeState_

In re: _Jane Public_
Petitioner

Case No:
Given by
Court Clerk

vs.

Richard Public
Respondent

SUMMONS: PERSONAL SERVICE ON AN INDIVIDUAL

TO: _Richard Public_
2200 SomeStreet, Othertown, SomeState 00005

IMPORTANT

A lawsuit has been filed against you. You have 20 calendar days after this summons is served on you to file a written response to the attached complaint/petition with the clerk of this circuit court. A phone call will not protect you. Your written response, including the case number given above and the names of the parties, must be filed if you want the court to hear your side of the case. If you do not file your written response on time, you may lose the case, and your wages, money, and property may thereafter be taken without further warning from the court. There are other legal requirements. You may want to call an attorney right away. If you do not know an attorney, you may call an attorney referral service or a legal aid office (listed in the phone book).

PROCESS SERVICE MEMORANDUM

TO: Sheriff of _SomeCounty_ County, State of _SomeState_,
SomeDivision Division:

RE: _Jane Public_ , Petitioner
and _Richard Public_ , Respondent
SomeCourt Circuit Court, County of _SomeCounty_
Case No. _Given By Court Clerk_
Please serve the Summons and Petition herein, in the above-styled cause upon:

Respondent: _Richard Public_
Home Address: _2200 SomeStreet_
Othertown, SomeState 00005
Work Address: _1900 SomeStreet_
Anytown, SomeState 00002

Thank you.

SPECIAL INSTRUCTIONS:

Signature of party
Jane Public
Printed name
1300 Somewhere St.,Anytown
Address
SomeState 00001
City   State   Zip
_(123)456-7890_
Telephone (area code and number)
_(123)456-7891_
Fax   (area code and number)

Process Service Memorandum

Since it is often impossible to serve the summons and petition personally, a process server may be called upon to deliver the document. Typically the county sheriff performs this task. This form provides the particulars for delivering the summons. The summons and the petition may be mailed to the sheriff's office in the county where your ex-spouse resides.

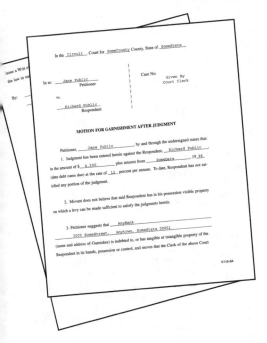

Motion for Garnishment After Judgment

With this form, the custodial parent asks the court to attach money that is not in the physical possession of the non-custodial parent. Money may be in bank or trust accounts, or it may be coming from judgments or insurance payoffs. (This form is not used for wage attachments.) If support payments are in arrears, first the court will determine the exact amount owed and a judgment will be entered for that amount. Upon determining that the money is not in the possession of the non-custodial parent, the court, using a writ of garnishment, will order the person or institution holding the money to pay it to the custodial parent.

Final Judgment Modifying Child Support

Child support payments may be modified to reflect changes in child support guidelines or changes in the circumstances of the parent(s). This form is used by the court when it decides to grant or deny a request for an increase or decrease in child support. If the court exceeds or fails to meet the guidelines, it must justify its decision with facts. Therefore, it is necessary to answer all questions truthfully and provide the court with full explanations. This form is completed by the court and signed by the judge.

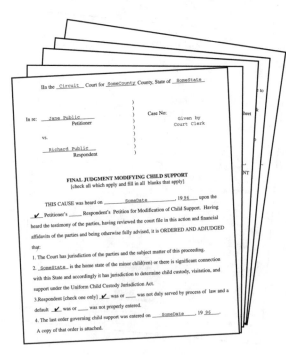

The forms in this guide

About These Made E-Z Forms:
While the legal forms and documents in this product generally conform to the requirements of courts nationwide, certain courts may have additional requirements. Before completing and filing the forms in this product, check with the clerk of the court concerning these requirements.

NOTICE

Before you submit any forms, make copies and use them as worksheets. They will help familiarize you with the type of information you may be required to provide. Because each state may have different requirements, you may need additional forms. Therefore, before you submit any forms, you must contact the appropriate state agency for specific requirements.

In the _____ Court for _____ County, State of _____

In re: _____   )
Petitioner

vs.

_____
Respondent

)
)
)   Case No:
)
)
)   Division:
)
)
)

UNIFORM SUPPORT PETITION

1. This petition of petitioner, _____ (name), respectfully shows the court that this petition is for [check all that apply]:

_____ Support   _____ Medical coverage   _____ Arrearage

_____ Reimbursement   _____ Establishment of paternity

_____ A Paternity Affidavit is attached for reference

_____ The General Testimony for URESA is attached for reference

2. Petitioner, _____ (name), resides at _____

_____ (address) and has custody of the following dependents of the respondent:

Names   Date of Birth

_____   _____

_____   _____

_____   _____

3. Petitioner and the respondent were [check one only]:

    ____ Never married to each other.

    ____ Married on this _____ (day) of _____ (month), _____ (year).

    ____ Divorce is pending (date filed _____) in _____ County,

    _____ (State).

    ____ Divorced on _____ (day) of _____ (month), _____ (year) in

    _____ County, _____ (State).

4. Respondent resides at:

    _____

    _____

    Respondent's last known employer and address of employer is

    _____

    _____

    _____

5. The dependents are entitled to support and/or medical coverage from the respondent. Respondent has a legal obligation to pay support pursuant to the laws of the initiating state, which is enforceable under the following reciprocal support status reference: _____.

6. Since the date of _____ respondent has not provided support for the named dependents.

7. a. ____ The respondent is not under a court order to pay child support.

    b. ____ The respondent is under a court order to pay support (see attached order).

    c. ____ The respondent should pay the amount of ongoing support for the dependents in an amount as permitted by the law of the responding state.

Wherefore, the petitioner requests an order for the following: [check all that apply]

    ____ Child support in the amount prescribed by law.

    ____ Registration and enforcement of the attached current support order.

    ____ Medical coverage.

_____ Arrearage as prescribed by law from the date of _____.

_____ Payment of costs and attorney's fees by the respondent.

Under penalties of perjury, all information and facts stated in this petition are true to the best of my knowledge and belief.

By: _____ (signed)

_____ (printed)

STATE OF _____

COUNTY OF_____

Sworn to (or affirmed) and subscribed before me on_____ , _____ (year)

by_____.

Witness my hand and official seal.

_____
Signature of Notary

Affiant: _____Known _____Produced ID

Type of ID _____

IF A NONLAWYER HELPED YOU FILL OUT THIS FORM HE/SHE MUST FILL IN THE BLANKS BELOW. [FILL IN ALL BLANKS]

I, (name of nonlawyer)_____, a nonlawyer, located at

(street)_____ (city)_____ (state)_____,

(phone)_____, helped (name)_____, who is the

(petitioner) (respondent), fill out this form.

In the _____ Court for _____ County, State of _____

In re: _____   )
                        Petitioner   )   Case No:
)
        vs.   )   Division:
)
    _____   )
                        Respondent   )

SUMMONS: PERSONAL SERVICE ON AN INDIVIDUAL

TO:_____

_____

IMPORTANT

A lawsuit has been filed against you. You have 20 calendar days after this summons is served on you to file a written response to the attached complaint/petition with the clerk of this circuit court. A phone call will not protect you. Your written response, including the case number given above and the names of the parties, must be filed if you want the court to hear your side of the case. If you do not file your written response on time, you may lose the case, and your wages, money, and property may thereafter be taken without further warning from the court. There are other legal requirements. You may want to call an attorney right away. If you do not know an attorney, you may call an attorney referral service or a legal aid office (listed in the phone book).

If you choose to file a written response yourself, at the same time you file your written response to the court you must also mail or take a copy of your written response to the person named below.

WARNING: The State of _____ requires that you provide to the other party in this lawsuit access to or copies of certain documents and information. Failure to do this can result in the court taking action against you, including dismissal (throwing out your case) or striking of pleadings (throwing out part of your case).

Petitioner
_____

Mailing Address
_____

City/State/Zip Code
_____

THE STATE OF _____

TO EACH SHERIFF OF THE STATE: You are commanded to serve this summons and a copy

of the complaint in this lawsuit on the above-named defendant.

DATED: _____

            _____

            As Clerk of the Court

By: _____

            Deputy Clerk

PROCESS SERVICE MEMORANDUM

TO: Sheriff of _____ County, State of _____, _____ Division:

RE: _____, Petitioner

and

_____, Respondent

_____Circuit Court, County of _____

Case No. _____

Please serve the Summons and Petition herein, in the above-styled cause upon:

Respondent: _____

Home Address: _____

_____

Work Address: _____

_____

Thank you.

SPECIAL INSTRUCTIONS:

_____
Signature of party

_____
Printed name

_____
Address

_____
City   State   Zip

_____
Telephone (area code and number)

_____
Fax (area code and number)

In the _____ Court for _____ County, State of _____

In re: _____   )   Case No:
            Petitioner

In re: _____)
                    Petitioner   )   Case No:
)
  vs.   )   Division:
)
_____)
                    Respondent)

NON-MILITARY AFFIDAVIT

STATE OF _____)

                        SS # of Respondent:

COUNTY OF _____)

      BEFORE ME, the undersigned authority, personally appeared _____,

who upon oath, deposes and says:

1. I am the Petitioner (or Attorney of record for the Petitioner, if represented) in the above-

styled cause.

2. Based upon information, I state that the Respondent,_____, is not at the pre-

sent time in the military services of the United States or any of its allies.

      FURTHER AFFIANT SAYETH NOT.

By: _____ (signed)

        _____ (printed)

STATE OF _____

COUNTY OF_____

Sworn to (or affirmed) and subscribed before me on_____, _____ (year)

by_____.

Witness my hand and official seal.

_____

Signature of Notary

Affiant: _____Known   _____Produced ID

Type of ID _____

IF A NONLAWYER HELPED YOU FILL OUT THIS FORM HE/SHE MUST FILL IN
THE BLANKS BELOW. [FILL IN ALL BLANKS]

I, (name of nonlawyer)_____, a nonlawyer, located at

(street)_____ (city)_____ (state)_____,

(phone)_____, helped (name)_____, who is the

(petitioner) (respondent), fill out this form.

In the _____ Court for _____ County, State of _____

In re: _____	)	Case No:
	)	
Petitioner	)	
	)	
vs.	)	Division:
	)	
_____	)	
Respondent	)	

FINANCIAL AFFIDAVIT (SHORT FORM)

STATE OF _____

COUNTY OF_____

BEFORE ME, this day personally appeared _____, who being duly sworn, deposes and says that the following information is true and correct according to his/her best knowledge and belief.

EMPLOYMENT AND INCOME

OCCUPATION: _____

EMPLOYED BY: _____

ADDRESS:_____

SOC. SEC. NO. _____

DATE OF BIRTH: _____

PAY PERIOD: _____

RATE OF PAY: _____

If you are employed but expecting soon to become unemployed or change jobs, describe the change you expect and why and how it will affect your income. If currently unemployed, describe your efforts to find employment, how soon you expect to be employed, and the pay you expect to receive.

_____

_____

Business income from sources such as self-employment, partnerships, close corporations, and/or independent contracts (gross receipts minus ordinary and necessary expenses required to produce income.) _____

Disability benefits _____

Workers' compensation _____

Unemployment compensation _____

Pension, retirement or annuity payments _____

Social Security benefits _____

Spousal support received from previous marriage _____

Interest and dividends _____

Rental income (gross receipts minus ordinary any necessary expenses required to produce income) _____

Income from royalties, trusts or estates _____

Reimbursed expenses and in kind payments to the extent that they reduce personal living expenses _____

Gains derived from dealing in property (not including non-recurring gains) _____

Itemize any other income of a recurring nature _____

TOTAL MONTHLY INCOME $_____

LESS MONTHLY DEDUCTIONS

Federal, state and local income taxes (corrected for filing status and actual number of withholding allowances) _____

FICA or self-employment tax (annualized) _____

Mandatory union dues _____

Mandatory retirement _____

Health insurance payments _____
Court-ordered support payments for the children actually paid _____

TOTAL DEDUCTIONS $_____

TOTAL NET INCOME $_____

AVERAGE MONTHLY EXPENSES
HOUSEHOLD:

Mortgage or rent payments   _____

Property taxes   _____

Insurance   _____

Electricity   _____

Waste, garbage and sewer   _____

Telephone   _____

Fuel   _____

Barber/beauty parlor   _____

Cosmetics/toiletries   _____

Holiday gifts   _____

Other expenses: _____   _____

TOTAL MONTHLY PAYMENTS TO CREDITORS $_____

TOTAL MONTHLY EXPENSES $_____

ASSETS (Ownership: If marital, put one-half of the total value under petitioner, and one-half under respondent no matter whose name the item is in.)

DESCRIPTION	VALUE	PETITIONER	RESPONDENT
Cash on hand	_____	_____	_____
Cash in banks	_____	_____	_____
Stocks/bonds	_____	_____	_____
Notes	_____	_____	_____
Real estate:			
Homes:			
_____	_____	_____	_____
_____	_____	_____	_____
Automobiles:			
_____	_____	_____	_____
_____	_____	_____	_____

Other personal property:

  Contents of home   _____   _____   _____

  Jewelry   _____   _____   _____

  Life Ins./ cash
  surrender value   _____   _____   _____

Other assets:

_____   _____   _____   _____

_____   _____   _____   _____

TOTAL ASSETS $_____ $_____ $_____

LIABILITIES

Creditor	Security	Balance	Husband	Wife
_____	_____	_____	_____	_____
_____	_____	_____	_____	_____
_____	_____	_____	_____	_____
_____	_____	_____	_____	_____

TOTAL LIABILITIES $_____

STATE OF _____

COUNTY OF_____

Sworn to (or affirmed) and subscribed before me on_____, _____ (year)

by_____.

Witness my hand and official seal.

        _____
        Signature of Notary

        Affiant: _____Known _____Produced ID
        Type of ID _____

IF A NONLAWYER HELPED YOU FILL OUT THIS FORM HE/SHE MUST FILL IN THE BLANKS BELOW. [FILL IN ALL BLANKS]

I, (name of nonlawyer)_____, a nonlawyer, located at

(street)_____ (city)_____ (state)_____,

(phone)_____, helped (name)_____, who is the

(petitioner) (respondent), fill out this form.

In the _____ Court for _____ County, State of _____

In re: _____	))) Case No:
Petitioner	))
vs.	) Division:
_____	)))
Respondent	)

MOTION FOR HEALTH INSURANCE COVERAGE

1. On _____ _____ (year), this court ordered the child(ren)'s [check one only] _____ father or _____ mother to provide health insurance coverage for the following child(ren):

Name	Date of Birth	Age	Soc. Sec. No.
_____	_____	_____	_____
_____	_____	_____	_____
_____	_____	_____	_____
_____	_____	_____	_____
_____	_____	_____	_____

2. Notice to [check one only] ____ Petitioner or ____ Respondent: [check one only]

    ____ a. On _____, which is at least 15 days before filing this application, I gave written notice of my intent to seek this order to _____ by [check one only] ____certified mail ____personal service.

_____ b. The requirement of written notice has been waived by the other party.

3. I ask the court to order the employer, or other person providing health insurance coverage to enroll or maintain the child(ren) on any health insurance coverage available to father/mother.

I CERTIFY THAT THE MOTION FOR HEALTH INSURANCE COVERAGE WAS:

[check one only] _____ mailed, _____telefaxed and mailed, or _____ hand delivered to the person(s) listed below on _____, _____ (year).

Party or their attorney (if represented)   Other

Name_____   Name_____

Address _____   Address _____

_____   _____
City   State   Zip   City   State   Zip

Telephone _____   Telephone _____

Fax _____   Fax _____

DATED:_____

_____
Signature of party signing certificate and pleading

Printed name_____

Address_____

_____
City   State   Zip

_____
Telephone (area code and number)

_____
Fax (area code and number)

94

STATE OF _____

COUNTY OF_____

Sworn to (or affirmed) and subscribed before me on_____, _____ (year)

by_____.

Witness my hand and official seal.

_____
Signature of Notary

Affiant: _____Known _____Produced ID

Type of ID _____

IF A NONLAWYER HELPED YOU FILL OUT THIS FORM HE/SHE MUST FILL IN
THE BLANKS BELOW. [FILL IN ALL BLANKS]

I, (name of nonlawyer)_____, a nonlawyer, located at

(street)_____ (city)_____ (state)_____,

(phone)_____, helped (name)_____, who is the

(petitioner) (respondent), fill out this form.

In the _____ Court for _____ County, State of _____

In re: _____)
)
                Petitioner)

In re:	_____)	Case No:
	Petitioner)	
	)	
vs.	)	Division:
	)	
	_____)	
	Respondent)	

FINAL JUDGMENT MODIFYING CHILD SUPPORT
[check all which apply and fill in all blanks that apply]

THIS CAUSE was heard on _____, _____ (year) upon the _____ Petitioner's _____ Respondent's Petition for Modification of Child Support. Having heard the testimony of the parties, having reviewed the court file in this action and financial affidavits of the parties and being otherwise fully advised, it is ORDERED AND ADJUDGED THAT:

1. The Court has jurisdiction of the parties and the subject matter of this proceeding.

2. _____ is the home state of the minor child(ren) or there is significant connection with this State and accordingly it has jurisdiction to determine child custody, visitation, and support under the Uniform Child Custody Jurisdiction Act.

3. Respondent [check one only] _____ was or _____ was not duly served by process of law and a default _____ was or _____ was not properly entered.

4. The last order governing child support was entered on _____, _____ (year). A copy of that order is attached.

5. There [check one only] _____ has or _____ has not been a substantial change in the circumstances of the parties since the entry of the last order governing child support, specifically:

_____

_____

_____

_____

_____.

6. It [check one only] _____ is or _____ is not in the best interest of the minor child(ren) that the current child support order be changed because:

_____

_____

_____

_____.

7. Child Support [fill in all blanks that apply]

    a.   Petitioner's net income is: _____. OR

         Petitioner's imputed net income is: _____, based upon the following:

_____

_____.

    b.   Respondent's net income is: _____. OR

         Respondent's imputed net income is: _____ based upon the following:

_____

_____.

[check all that apply]

    _____ c.   Child support should be set by the child support guidelines of _____.

    _____ d.   The calculations and conclusion included in the child support guidelines worksheet, filed in this case by [check one only] _____ petitioner or _____ respondent, are adopted by this court and incorporated in this order.

97

THE COURT MUST MAKE SPECIFIC, WRITTEN FINDINGS WHY AWARDING THE AMOUNT OF CHILD SUPPORT REQUIRED BY _____ STATUTES WOULD BE UNJUST OR INAPPROPRIATE IF THE AMOUNT AWARDED IS DIFFERENT FROM THE GUIDELINES AMOUNT BY PLUS OR MINUS FIVE PERCENT (5%).

_____ e.   Child support should not be set by the child support guidelines of _____. The basis for ordering [check one only] _____ more or _____ less than the guidelines amount of child support pursuant to _____ Statutes is:

_____

_____

_____

_____

_____

_____

_____.

f.   Past Due Child Support/Arrearages. The [check one only] _____ petitioner or _____ respondent has a total child support arrearage of $_____, this is based upon payments missed on the following dates in the following amounts:

_____

_____

_____.

g.   _____Medical insurance [check one only] ___is or ____is not reasonably available to the [check one only] _____ petitioner or _____ respondent for the child(ren) and [check one only] _____ petitioner or _____ respondent should be required to provide it.

h.   _____Dental insurance [check one only] ___is or ____is not reasonably available to the [check one only] _____ petitioner or _____ respondent for the child(ren) and the [check one only] _____ petitioner or _____ respondent should be required to provide it.

8. THE COURT MUST MAKE SPECIFIC, WRITTEN FINDINGS OF FACT EXPLAINING WHY ATTORNEYS' FEES ARE BEING GRANTED AND EXPLAINING THE BASIS OF THE AMOUNT AWARDED.

1. The [check one only] ____husband's or ____wife's request for fees and costs is DENIED.

2. The [check one only] ____husband's or ____wife's request for fees and costs is GRANTED.

[check all that apply]

_____ Attorneys' fees, _____ suit money, and/or _____ costs be awarded to

[check one only] _____ petitioner or _____ respondent.

The basis for granting this award and for the determination of the amount is:

_____

_____

_____

_____

_____

_____

_____.

Therefore, upon consideration of the above findings, it is hereby ORDERED AND ADJUDGED that:

A. The Petition/Request to Modify Child Support is [check one only] _____GRANTED or _____ DENIED.

B. Child Support

1. _____Child support of $_____ to be paid by the [check one only] _____petitioner or _____ respondent [check one only] _____weekly _____biweekly _____twice a month _____monthly.

This support shall continue until the first of the parties' minor children reaches the age of 18, or if the child(ren) are between the ages of 18 and 19 and are still in high school performing in good faith with a reasonable expectation of graduation, until the child(ren) reaches the age of 19. At that time the child support will be recomputed under the then-current Child Support Guidelines.

2. _____ The [check one only] ____petitioner or ____respondent shall pay the sum of

$_____ per _____ for _____ children, for past due child support. This payment for past due child support shall last for _____ months/years, until all past due support and interest are paid. Interest on past due child support shall be added to obligor's debt at the rate of _____% per annum until paid.

3. _____Unusual or uninsured medical/dental expenses for the children be provided by: [check one only] _____ petitioner or _____ respondent or _____ petitioner and respondent each pay one-half.

4. _____Medical insurance to be provided by [check one only] _____ petitioner or _____ respondent for the child(ren).

5. _____ Dental insurance to be provided by [check one only] _____ petitioner or _____ respondent for the child(ren).

6. _____ Life insurance shall be maintained for the benefit of the minor child(ren) as beneficiaries or as stated in the [name trust] _____ for the benefit of the minor children created _____, _____ (year) with the [check one only] _____ petitioner or _____ respondent or other [specify]_____ as owner as follows: [check one only] _____none ordered or _____by petitioner with a benefit amount of $_____ or _____ by respondent with a benefit amount of $_____.

7. All payments of child support and alimony shall be as follows: [check all which apply]

_____ Directly to the person the court has ordered will be paid the support

_____ Payment will be through the Central Depository by the attached order Family Law Form.

_____ Payment will be by the attached Family Law Form income deduction order.

C. _____ Attorneys' fees, suit money, and costs be awarded to: [check one only] _____ petitioner or _____ respondent in the amount of $_____(fees), $_____ (costs), and $_____ suit money. The basis for granting or denying this award and for the amount of any fees and costs awarded is given in the findings of fact in this judgment.

D. This court awards the petitioner the following further relief in this cause:

_____

_____

F. The court reserves jurisdiction to enforce the terms of this order and all documents incorporated into it (e.g., parties' stipulation/agreement, child support guidelines worksheet, etc.).

DONE and ORDERED in _____ County, State of _____, on _____, _____ (year).

_____
CIRCUIT JUDGE

cc:

Party or their attorney (if represented)

Name_____

Address_____

_____
City   State   Zip

Telephone _____

Fax _____

Respondent or their attorney (if represented)

Name_____

Address_____

_____
City   State   Zip

Telephone _____

Fax _____

Other

Name_____

Address_____

_____
City   State   Zip

Telephone _____

Fax _____

Glossary of useful terms

-A-

Administrative Procedure

The method by which support orders are made and enforced by an executive agency rather than by courts and judges.

Aid to Families with Dependent Children (AFDC)

Assistance payments made on behalf of children who don't have the financial support of one of their parents by reason of death, disability, or continued absence from the home; known in many states as ADC.

Aid to Dependent Children Arrearages

Unpaid child support for past periods owed by a parent who is obligated to pay an assignment of support. A person receiving public assistance agrees to turn over to the state any rights to child support, including arrearages, paid by the obligated parent in exchange for receipt of an AFDC grant and other benefits.

Arrearage

An unpaid and overdue debt; when child support has not been paid, it is said to be "in arrears" and the amount owed is the "arrearage."

-C-

Complaint

A written document filed in court in which the person initiating the action names the persons, allegations, and relief sought.

Consent Agreement

A voluntarily written admission of paternity or responsibility for support.

Custodial Parent

A person with legal custody and with whom the child lives; may be parent, other relative, or someone else.

Custody

Legal determination which establishes with whom a child shall live.

-D-

Default

The failure of a defendant to file an answer, response, or appeal in a judicial proceeding after having been served with a summons and complaint.

Default Judgment

The decision made by the court when the defendant (respondent) fails to respond.

-E-

Electronic Funds Transfer

The transfer of money from one bank account directly to another or to a child support enforcement agency.

Enforcement

Obtaining payment of a child support or medical support obligation.

-F-

Federal Parent Locator Service (FPLS)

A service operated by the Federal Office of Service Child Support Enforcement to help the states locate parents to obtain child support payments; also used in cases of parental kidnapping related to custody and visitation determinations; FPLS obtains address and employer information from Federal agencies.

-G-

Garnishment

A legal proceeding under which part of a person's wages and/or assets is withheld for payment of a debt.

Genetic Testing

The analysis of inherited factors (usually by blood test) of mother, child and alleged father which can help to prove or disprove that a particular man fathered a particular child.

Guidelines

A standard method for setting child support obligations based on the income of the parent(s) and other factors as determined by state law.

-I-

Interstate

Existing or occurring between two or more states.

Intrastate

Existing or occurring within a state.

-J-

Jurisdiction

The legal authority which a court has over particular persons and certain types of cases in a defined geographical area.

-L-

Legal Father

A man who is recognized by law as the male parent.

Lien

A claim upon property to prevent sale or transfer until a debt is satisfied.

Long-Arm Statute

A law which permits one state to claim personal jurisdiction over someone who lives in another state.

-M-

Medicaid Program

A federally funded medical support program for low income families.

Medical Support

The legal provision for payment of medical and dental bills; can be linked to a parent's access to medical insurance.

-N-

Non-Custodial Parent

A parent who does not have primary custody of a child but who has a responsibility for financial support.

-O-

Obligation

The amount of money to be paid as support by the responsible parent and the manner by which it is to be paid.

Offset

The amount of money taken from a parent's state or federal income tax refund to satisfy a child support debt.

Order

The direction of a magistrate, judge or properly empowered administrative officer.

-P-

Paternity Judgement

The legal determination of fatherhood.

Petitioner (Plaintiff)

The person who brings an action or complaint to court, or who sues in a civil case.

Presumption of Paternity

A rule of law under which evidence of a man's paternity (e.g. voluntary acknowledgment, genetic test results) creates a presumption that the man is the father of a child. A refutable presumption can be challenged by evidence that the man is not the father, but it shifts the burden of proof to the father to disprove paternity.

Probability of Paternity

The probability that the alleged father is the biological father of the child as indicated by genetic test results.

Public Assistance

The money granted from the state/federal Aid to Families with Dependent Children program to a person or family for living expenses; eligibility based on need.

-R-

Respondent (Defendant)

The person against whom a civil or criminal proceeding is begun.

-S-

State Parent Locator

A service operated by the State Child Support Service (SPLS) enforcement agencies to locate non-custodial parents to establish paternity, and establish and enforce child support obligations.

Stay

The act of stopping a judicial proceeding by an order of a court.

-U-

Uniform Interstate Family Support Act (UIFSA)

Laws enacted at the state level which provide mechanisms for establishing and enforcing support obligations across state lines by allowing one state, through the use of long-arm statutes, to assert personal jurisdiction over a non-custodial parent in another state.

Uniform Reciprocal Enforcement of Support Act (URESA)

Laws allowing for state-to-state cooperation in the establishing and enforcing of support obligations when the non-custodial parent lives in one state and the custodial parent and child(ren) live in another.

-V-

Visitation

The right of a non-custodial parent to visit or spend time with his or her children following separation or divorce.

Voluntary Acknowledgement of Paternity

An acknowledgement by a man, or both parents, that the man is the father of a child, usually provided in writing on an affidavit or form.

-W-

Wage Attachment (Wage Withholding)

The procedure by which automatic deductions are made from wage or income to pay some debt such as child support; may be voluntary or involuntary.

Resources

STATE CHILD SUPPORT ENFORCEMENT OFFICES

ALABAMA

Intrastate/Interstate Contact:
Department of Human Resources
Division of Child Support
50 Ripley Street
Montgomery, AL 36130-1801
(334) 242-9300
FAX: (334) 242-0606

ALASKA

Intrastate/Interstate Contact:
Child Support Enforcement Division
550 West 7th Avenue, 4th Floor
Anchorage, AK 99501-6699
(907) 269-6829
FAX: (907) 269-6914

ARIZONA

Intrastate Contact:
Division of Child Support
Enforcement
P.O. Box 3822
Phoenix, AZ 85030
(602) 252-4045
FAX: (602)248-3126

Interstate Contact:
P.O. Box 40458
Phoenix, AZ 85067
(602) 274-7951
FAX: (602) 274-8250

ARKANSAS

Intrastate/Interstate Contact:
Office of Child Support Enforcement
P.O. Box 8133
Little Rock, AR 72203
(501) 682-8710
FAX: (501) 682-6002

CALIFORNIA

Intrastate Contact:
Department of Justice
Child Support Program
P.O. Box 944255
Sacramento, CA 94244-2550
(916) 324-5173
FAX: (916) 324-9260

Interstate Contact:
Department of Social Services
P.O. Box 944245
Sacramento, CA 94244-2450
(916) 654-1273
FAX: (916)657-2074

COLORADO

Intrastate/Interstate Contact:
Division of Child Support
Enforcement
1575 Sherman Street, 2nd Floor
Denver, CO 80203-1714
(303) 866-5965
FAX: (303) 866-2214

CONNECTICUT

Intrastate/Interstate Contact:
Support Enforcement Division
287 Main Street
East Hartford, CT 06118-1885
(860) 569-6233
FAX: (860) 569-6557

DELAWARE

Intrastate/Interstate Contact:
Division of Child Support
Enforcement
P.O. Box 904
New Castle, DE 19720
(302) 577-4804
FAX: (302) 577-4873

DISTRICT OF COLUMBIA

Intrastate Contact:
Office of Paternity and
Child Support Enforcement
800 9th Street, S.W., 2nd Floor
Washington, DC 20024-2485
(202) 724-8800

Interstate Contact:
(202) 645-5355

FLORIDA

Intrastate Contact:
Child Support Enforcement Program
Department of Revenue
P.O. Box 8030
Tallahassee, FL 32314-8030
(904) 922-9564
FAX: (904) 921-5727

Interstate Contact:
(904) 922-9715
FAX: (904) 488-4401

GEORGIA

Intrastate/Interstate Contact:
Locate/Central Registry Manager
P.O. Box 38070
Atlanta, GA 30334-0070
(404) 657-3784
FAX: (404) 657-1462

GUAM

Intrastate/Interstate Contact:
Department of Law
Child Support Enforcement Office
238 Archbishop F.C. Flores, 7th Floor
Agana, GU 96910
011 (671) 475-3360

HAWAII

Intrastate/Interstate Contact:
Child Support Enforcement Agency
680 Iwilet Street, Suite 490
Honolulu, HI 96817
(808) 587-3717
FAX: (808) 587-3775

IDAHO

Intrastate/Interstate Contact:
Idaho Interstate/Central Registry
Service
P.O. Box 83720
Boise, ID 83720 - 0036
(208) 334-5710
FAX: (208) 334-0666

ILLINOIS

Intrastate/Interstate Contact:
Illinois Central Registry
P.O. Box 19405
Springfield, IL 62794-9405
(217) 782-0420
FAX: (217) 524-6049

INDIANA

Intrastate/Interstate Contact:
Child Support Bureau
402 West Washington Street
Rm W360
Indianapolis, IN 46204
(317) 232-3447
FAX: (317) 233-4925

IOWA

Intrastate Contact:
Bureau of Collections
Hoover State Office Bldg., Fl 5 SW
1305 E. Walnut Street
Des Moines, IA 50319
(515) 281-5580
FAX: (515) 281-8854

Interstate Contact:
211 E. Maple Street, Suite 100
Des Moines, IA 50309
(515) 242-6099
FAX: (515) 281-6632

KANSAS

Intrastate/Interstate Contact:
CSE Central Office
P.O. Box 497
Topeka, KS 66601-0497
(913) 296-3237
FAX: (913) 296-5206

KENTUCKY

Intrastate/Interstate Contact:
Division of Child Support
Enforcement
275 East Main Street
Frankfort, KY 40621
(502) 564-2285
FAX: (502) 564-5988

LOUISIANA

Intrastate/Interstate Contact:
Support Enforcement Services
Office of Family Support
P.O. Box 94065
Baton Rouge, LA 70804-4065
(504) 342-4780
FAX: (504) 342-7397

MAINE

Intrastate/Interstate Contact:
Division of Support Enforcement
and Recovery
Department of Human Services
Whitten Road, State House Station 11
Augusta, ME 04333
(207) 287-2886
FAX: (207) 287-5096

MARYLAND

Intrastate/Interstate Contact:
Child Support Enforcement
Administration
311 West Saratoga Street, Rm 313
Baltimore, MD 21201
(410) 767-7682
FAX: (410) 333-8992

MASSACHUSETTS

Intrastate Contact:
Department of Revenue
Child Support Enforcement Division
27 Water Street
Wakefield, MA 01880
(617) 246-0774

Interstate Contact:
141 Portland Street
Cambridge, MA 02139
(617) 577-7200

MICHIGAN

Intrastate Contact:
Office of Child Support
Family Independence Agency
7109 W. Saginaw Hwy.
P.O. Box 30478
Lansing, MI 48909-7978
(517) 335-3486

Interstate Contact:
(517) 335-0892

MINNESOTA

Intrastate/Interstate Contact:
Child Support Enforcement Division
Department of Human Services
444 Lafayette Road
St. Paul, MN 55155-3846
(612) 297-5846
FAX: (612) 297-4450

MISSISSIPPI

Intrastate/Interstate Contact:
Division of Child Support
Enforcement
Department of Human Services
P.O. Box 352
Jackson, MS 39205
(601) 359-4869
FAX: (601) 359-4415

MISSOURI

Intrastate Contact:
Department of Social Services
Division of Child Support
Enforcement
2701 West Main, P.O. Box 1468
Jefferson City, MO 65102-1468
(573) 751-4224
FAX: (573) 751-1257

Interstate Contact:
227 Metro Drive
P.O. Box 1527
Jefferson City, MO 65102-1527
(573) 751-4301
FAX: (573) 751-8450

MONTANA

Intrastate/Interstate Contact:
Child Support Enforcement Division
Department of Public Health
and Human Services
P.O. Box 202943
Helena, MT 59620
(406) 444-4614
FAX: (406) 444-1370

NEBRASKA

Intrastate/Interstate Contact:
Child Support Enforcement Office
Department of Social Services
P.O. Box 95026
Lincoln, NE 68509
(402) 471-9103
FAX: (402) 471-9455

NEVADA

Intrastate/Interstate Contact:
Child Support Enforcement Program
2527 North Carson Street
Carson City, NV 89710
(702) 687-4744
(702) 687-5080

NEW HAMPSHIRE

Intrastate Contact:
Office of Child Support
6 Hazen Drive
Concord, NH 03301
(603) 271-4428
FAX: (603) 271-4771

Interstate Contact:
(603) 271-4440

NEW JERSEY

Intrastate/Interstate Contact:
Department of Human Services
Bureau of Child Support and
Paternity Programs
CN 716
Trenton, NJ 08625-0716
(609) 588-2915
FAX: (609) 588-2354

NEW MEXICO

Intrastate/Interstate Contact:
Central Registry
P.O. Box 25109
Santa Fe, NM 87505
(505) 827-7200
FAX: (505) 827-7285

NEW YORK

Intrastate/Interstate Contact:
Office of Child Support Enforcement
P.O. Box 14
One Commerce Plaza
Albany, NY 12260
(518) 474-1078
FAX: (518) 486-3127

NORTH CAROLINA

Intrastate/Interstate Contact:
Child Support Enforcement Section
Division of Social Services
100 East Six Forks Road
Raleigh, NC 27609-7750
(919) 571-4114
FAX: (919) 571-4126

NORTH DAKOTA

Intrastate/Interstate Contact:
Child Support Enforcement Agency
P.O. Box 7190
Bismarck, ND 58507-7190
(701) 328-3582
FAX: (701) 328-5497

OHIO

Intrastate/Interstate Contact:
Office of Child Support Enforcement
Office of Family Assistance & Child
Support
30 East Broad Street, 31st Floor
Columbus, OH 43266-0423
(614) 752-6567
FAX: (614) 466-6613

OKLAHOMA

Intrastate/Interstate Contact:
Child Support Enforcement Division
P.O. Box 53552
Oklahoma City, OK 73125
Street Address: 2409 N. Kelley Avenue
Oklahoma City, OK 73111
(405) 522-2550
FAX: (405) 522-4570

OREGON

Intrastate/Interstate Contact:
Central Operations
1495 Edgewater NW, Suite 290
Salem, OR 97304
(503) 986-6015
FAX: (503) 986-5996

PENNSYLVANIA

Intrastate/Interstate Contact:
Bureau of Child Support Enforcement
Central Registry
P.O. Box 8018
Harrisburg, PA 17105
(717) 772-4940
FAX: (717) 787-9706

PUERTO RICO

Intrastate/Interstate Contact:
Child Support Enforcement
Department of Social Services
P.O. Box 3349
San Juan, PR 00902-9938
Street Address: Majagua Street, Bldg. 2
Wing 4, 2nd Floor
Miramar, PR 00902-9938
(809) 722-4731
FAX: (809) 723-6187

RHODE ISLAND

Intrastate Contact:
Rhode Island Child Support Services
77 Dorrance Street
Providence, RI 02903
(401) 277-2847
FAX: (401) 277-6674

Interstate Contact:
600 New London Avenue
Cranston, RI 02920
(401) 464-2018

SOUTH CAROLINA

Intrastate/Interstate Contact:
Child Support Enforcement Division
P.O. Box 1469
Columbia, SC 29202-1469
Street Address: 3150 Harden Street
Columbia, SC 29202-1469
(803) 737-5875
FAX: (803) 737-3301

SOUTH DAKOTA

Intrastate/Interstate Contact:
Department of Social Services
700 Governor's Drive
Pierre, SD 57501-2291
(605) 773-3641
FAX: (605) 773-6834

TENNESSEE

Intrastate/Interstate Contact:
Child Support Services
400 Deadrick Street, 12th Floor
Nashville, TN 37248-7400
(615) 313-4880
FAX: (615) 532-2791

TEXAS

Intrastate/Interstate Contact:
Office of the Attorney General
Child Support Division
P.O. Box 12017
Austin, TX 78711-2017
(512) 463-2181
FAX: (512) 476-1017

UTAH

Intrastate/Interstate Contact:
Office of Recovery Services
P.O. Box 45011
Salt Lake City, UT 84145-0011
(801) 536-8500
FAX: (801) 536-8509

VERMONT

Intrastate Contact:
Office of Child Support
103 South Main Street
Waterbury, VT 05671-1901
(802) 241-2319
FAX: (802) 244-1483

Interstate Contact:
(802) 241-2891

VIRGIN ISLANDS

Intrastate/Interstate Contact:
Paternity and Child Support Division
Department of Justice
GERS Building, 2nd Floor
48B-50C Krondprans Gade
St. Thomas, VI 00802
(809) 774-5666
FAX: (809) 774-9710

VIRGINIA

Intrastate Contact:
SPLS/Central Registry
730 East Broad Street
Richmond, VA 23219
(804) 692-1428
FAX: (804) 692-1405
Interstate Contact:
(804) 692-2405

WASHINGTON

Intrastate/Interstate Contact:
Washington State Support Registry
P.O. Box 9008
Olympia, WA 98507-9008
(360) 586-2125
FAX: (360) 586-3094

WEST VIRGINIA

Intrastate/Interstate Contact:
Child Support Enforcement Division
Building 6, Room 817
State Capitol Complex
Charleston, WV 25305
(304) 558-3780
(304) 558-4092

WISCONSIN

Intrastate Contact:
Division of Economic Support
P.O. Box 7935, Room 382
Madison, WI 53707-7935
(608) 267-0924
FAX: (608) 267-2824

Interstate Contact:
(608) 267-9665

WYOMING

Intrastate/Interstate Contact:
Department of Family Services
Child Support Enforcement Section
Hathaway Building, Room 385
Cheyenne, WY 82002-0490
(307) 777-6948
FAX: (307) 777-3693

... REGIONAL CHILD SUPPORT ... ENFORCEMENT OFFICES

REGION I

Connecticut, Maine, Massachusetts, New Hampshire, Rhode Island, Vermont
OCSE Program Manager
Administration for Children and Families
John F. Kennedy Federal Building
Room 2000
Boston, MA 02203
(617) 565-2440

REGION II

New York, New Jersey, Puerto Rico, Virgin Islands
OCSE Program Manager
Administration for Children and Families
Federal Building, Room 4048
26 Federal Plaza
New York, NY 10278
(212) 264-2890

REGION III

Delaware, Maryland, Pennsylvania, Virginia, West Virginia, District Of Columbia
OCSE Program Manager
Administration for Children and Families
P.O. Box 8436
3535 Market Street, Room 4119 MS/15
Philadelphia, PA 19104
(215) 596-4136

REGION IV

Alabama, Florida, Georgia, Kentucky, Mississippi, North Carolina, South Carolina, Tennessee
OCSE Program Manager
Administration for Children and Families
101 Marietta Tower, Suite 821
Atlanta, GA 30323
(404) 331-2180

REGION V

Illinois, Indiana, Michigan, Minnesota, Ohio, Wisconsin
OCSE Program Manager
Administration for Children and Families
105 W. Adams Street, 20th Floor
Chicago, IL 60603
(312) 353-4237

REGION VI

Arkansas, Louisiana, New Mexico, Oklahoma, Texas
OCSE Program Manager
Administration for Children and Families
1200 Main Tower, Suite 1050
Mail Stop A2
Dallas, TX 75202
(214) 767-3749

REGION VII

Iowa, Kansas, Missouri, Nebraska
OCSE Program Manager
Administration for Children and Families
601 East 12th Street
Federal Building, Suite 276
Kansas City, MO 64106
(816) 426-3584

REGION VIII

Colorado, Montana, North Dakota, South Dakota, Utah, Wyoming
OCSE Program Manager
Administration for Children and Families
Federal Office Building, Room 325
1961 Stout Street
Denver, CO 80294
(303) 844-3100

REGION IX

Arizona, California, Hawaii, Nevada, Guam
OCSE Program Manager
Administration for Children and Families
50 United Nations Plaza
Mail Stop 351
San Francisco, CA 94102
(415) 556-5176

REGION X

Alaska, Idaho, Oregon, Washington
OCSE Program Manager
Administration for Children and Families
2201 Sixth Avenue
Mail Stop RX-70
Seattle, WA 98121
(206) 615-2547

••• Online Resources •••

Adult Children of Divorce

http://www.mindspring.com/~blittle/odosbucket/adoc/home.html

American Academy of Matrimonial Lawyers

http://www.aaml.org/

American Divorce Information Network

http://www.divorceonline.com

American Association for Marriage and Family Therapy

http://www.aamft.org/

Divorce+Plus

http://pages.prodigy.com/divorceplus

Divorce Central

http://www.divorcecentral.com

Divorce Helpline Webworks

http://www.divorcehelp.com

DivorceInfo.com

http://www.divorceinfo.com

DivorceNet

http://www.divorcenet.com

Divorce Source

http://www.divorcesource.com

Divorcing.com

http://www.divorcing.com

Flying Solo

http://www.flyingsolo.com

Divorce Support

http://divorcesupport.miningco.com

Internet Imagers
Divorce Resources on the Internet

http://www.iimagers.com/divorce-resources.html

Legal Information Institute

http://www.divorcesource.com/search/general/divorcelaws.html

Men's Defense Association

http://www.mensdefense.org

MoneyCentral Family

http://moneycentral.msn.com/quickref/quickref.asp?
Cat=1&Topic=3#b

National Council for the Divorced and Separated

http://www.ncds.org.uk

Parents Without Partners

http://www.parentswithoutpartners.org/

Talkway

http://decaf.talkway.com/cgi-bin/cgi?request=enter&group=alt.
support.divorce

Yahoo Business and Economics

http://dir.yahoo.com/Business_and_Economy/Companies/
Law/Family/Divorce

Yahoo Society and Culture — Relationships

http://dir.yahoo.com/Society_and_Culture/Relationships/Divorce

••• Legal Search Engines •••

◆ **All Law**

http://www.alllaw.com

◆ **American Law Sources On Line**

http://www.lawsource.com/also/searchfm.htm

◆ **Catalaw**

http://www.catalaw.com

◆ **FindLaw**

URL: http://www.findlaw.com

◆ **Hieros Gamos**

http://www.hg.org/hg.html

◆ **InternetOracle**

http://www.internetoracle.com/legal.htm

◆ **LawAid**

http://www.lawaid.com/search.html

◆ **LawCrawler**

http://www.lawcrawler.com

◆ **LawEngine, The**

http://www.fastsearch.com/law

◆ **LawRunner**

http://www.lawrunner.com

◆ **'Lectric Law Library**™

http://www.lectlaw.com

◆ **Legal Search Engines**

http://www.dreamscape.com/frankvad/search.legal.html

◆ **LEXIS/NEXIS Communications Center**

http://www.lexis-nexis.com/lncc/general/search.html

◆ **Meta-Index for U.S. Legal Research**

http://gsulaw.gsu.edu/metaindex

◆ **Seamless Website, The**

http://seamless.com

◆ **USALaw**

http://www.usalaw.com/linksrch.cfm

◆ **WestLaw**

http://westdoc.com (Registered users only. Fee paid service.)

••• State Bar Associations •••

ALABAMA

Alabama State Bar
415 Dexter Avenue
Montgomery, AL 36104
mailing address:
PO Box 671
Montgomery, AL 36101
(334) 269-1515

http://www.alabar.org

ALASKA

Alaska Bar Association
510 L Street No. 602
Anchorage, AK 99501
mailing address:
PO Box 100279
Anchorage, AK 99510

http://www.alaskabar.org

ARIZONA

State Bar of Arizona
111 West Monroe
Phoenix, AZ 85003-1742
(602) 252-4804

http://www.azbar.org

ARKANSAS

Arkansas Bar Association
400 West Markham
Little Rock, AR 72201
(501) 375-4605

http://www.arkbar.org

CALIFORNIA

State Bar of California
555 Franklin Street
San Francisco, CA 94102
(415) 561-8200

http://www.calbar.org

Alameda County Bar Association
http://www.acbanet.org

COLORADO

Colorado Bar Association
No. 950, 1900 Grant Street
Denver, CO 80203
(303) 860-1115

http://www.cobar.org

CONNECTICUT

Connecticut Bar Association
101 Corporate Place
Rocky Hill, CT 06067-1894
(203) 721-0025

http://www.ctbar.org

DELAWARE

Delaware State Bar Association
1225 King Street, 10th floor
Wilmington, DE 19801
(302) 658-5279
(302) 658-5278 (lawyer referral
service)

http://www.dsba.org

DISTRICT OF COLUMBIA

District of Columbia Bar
1250 H Street, NW, 6th Floor
Washington, DC 20005
(202) 737-4700

Bar Association of the District of
Columbia
1819 H Street, NW, 12th floor
Washington, DC 20006-3690
(202) 223-6600

http://www.badc.org

FLORIDA
The Florida Bar
The Florida Bar Center
650 Apalachee Parkway
Tallahassee, FL 32399-2300
(850) 561-5600

> *http://www.flabar.org*

GEORGIA
State Bar of Georgia
800 The Hurt Building
50 Hurt Plaza
Atlanta, GA 30303
(404) 527-8700

> *http://www.gabar.org*

HAWAII
Hawaii State Bar Association
1136 Union Mall
Penthouse 1
Honolulu, HI 96813
(808) 537-1868

> *http://www.hsba.org*

IDAHO
Idaho State Bar
PO Box 895
Boise, ID 83701
(208) 334-4500

> *http://www2.state.id.us/isb*

ILLINOIS
Illinois State Bar Association
424 South Second Street
Springfield, IL 62701
(217) 525-1760

> *http://www.illinoisbar.org*

INDIANA
Indiana State Bar Association
230 East Ohio Street
Indianapolis, IN 46204
(317) 639-5465

> *http://www.ai.org/isba*

IOWA
Iowa State Bar Association
521 East Locust
Des Moines, IA 50309
(515) 243-3179

> *http://www.iowabar.org*

KANSAS
Kansas Bar Association
1200 Harrison Street
Topeka, KS 66612-1806
(785) 234-5696

> *http://www.ksbar.org*

KENTUCKY
Kentucky Bar Association
514 West Main Street
Frankfort, KY 40601-1883
(502) 564-3795

> *http://www.kybar.org*

LOUISIANA
Louisiana State Bar Association
601 St. Charles Avenue
New Orleans, LA 70130
(504) 566-1600

> *http://www.lsba.org*

MAINE

Maine State Bar Association
124 State Street
PO Box 788
Augusta, ME 04330
(207) 622-7523

http://www.mainebar.org

MARYLAND

Maryland State Bar Association
520 West Fayette Street
Baltimore, MD 21201
(301) 685-7878

http://www.msba.org/msba

MASSACHUSETTS

Massachusetts Bar Association
20 West Street
Boston, MA 02111
(617) 542-3602
(617) 542-9103 (lawyer referral
service)

http://www.massbar.org

MICHIGAN

State Bar of Michigan
306 Townsend Street
Lansing, MI 48933-2083
(517) 372-9030

http://www.michbar.org

MINNESOTA

Minnesota State Bar Association
514 Nicollet Mall
Minneapolis, MN 55402
(612) 333-1183

http://www.mnbar.org

MISSISSIPPI

The Mississippi Bar
643 No. State Street
Jackson, Mississippi 39202
(601) 948-4471

http://www.msbar.org

MISSOURI

The Missouri Bar
P.O. Box 119, 326 Monroe
Jefferson City, Missouri 65102
(314) 635-4128

http://www.mobar.org

MONTANA

State Bar of Montana
46 North Main
PO Box 577
Helena, MT 59624
(406) 442-7660

http://www.montanabar.org

NEBRASKA

Nebraska State Bar Association
635 South 14th Street, 2nd floor
Lincoln, NE 68508
(402) 475-7091

http://www.nebar.com

NEVADA

State Bar of Nevada
201 Las Vegas Blvd.
Las Vegas, NV 89101
(702) 382-2200

http://www.nvbar.org

NEW HAMPSHIRE

New Hampshire Bar Association
112 Pleasant Street
Concord, NH 03301
(603) 224-6942

http://www.nhbar.org

NEW JERSEY

New Jersey State Bar Association
One Constitution Square
New Brunswick, NJ 08901-1500
(908) 249-5000

NEW MEXICO

State Bar of New Mexico
5121 Masthead N.E.
Albuquerque, NM 87125
mailing address:
PO Box 25883
Albuquerque, NM 87125
(505) 843-6132

http://www.nmbar.org

NEW YORK

New York State Bar Association
One Elk Street
Albany, NY 12207
(518) 463-3200

http://www.nysba.org

NORTH CAROLINA

North Carolina State Bar
208 Fayetteville Street Mall
Raleigh, NC 27601
mailing address:
PO Box 25908
Raleigh, NC 27611
(919) 828-4620

North Carolina Bar Association
1312 Annapolis Drive
Raleigh, NC 27608
mailing address:
PO Box 3688
Cary, NC 27519-3688
(919) 677-0561

http://www.ncbar.org

NORTH DAKOTA

State Bar Association of North Dakota
515 1/2 East Broadway, suite 101
Bismarck, ND 58501
mailing address:
PO Box 2136
Bismarck, ND 58502
(701) 255-1404

OHIO

Ohio State Bar Association
1700 Lake Shore Drive
Columbus, OH 43204
mailing address:
PO Box 16562
Columbus, OH 43216-6562
(614) 487-2050

http://www.ohiobar.org

OKLAHOMA

Oklahoma Bar Association
1901 North Lincoln
Oklahoma City, OK 73105
(405) 524-2365

http://www.okbar.org

OREGON

Oregon State Bar
5200 S.W. Meadows Road
PO Box 1689
Lake Oswego, OR 97035-0889
(503) 620-0222

http://www.osbar.org

PENNSYLVANIA

Pennsylvania Bar Association
100 South Street
PO Box 186
Harrisburg, PA 17108
(717) 238-6715

http://www.pabar.org

Pennsylvania Bar Institute
http://www.pbi.org

PUERTO RICO

Puerto Rico Bar Association
PO Box 1900
San Juan, Puerto Rico 00903
(787) 721-3358

RHODE ISLAND

Rhode Island Bar Association
115 Cedar Street
Providence, RI 02903
(401) 421-5740

http://www.ribar.org

SOUTH CAROLINA

South Carolina Bar
950 Taylor Street
PO Box 608
Columbia, SC 29202
(803) 799-6653

http://www.scbar.org

SOUTH DAKOTA

State Bar of South Dakota
222 East Capitol
Pierre, SD 57501
(605) 224-7554

http://www.sdbar.org

TENNESSEE

Tennessee Bar Assn
3622 West End Avenue
Nashville, TN 37205
(615) 383-7421

http://www.tba.org

TEXAS

State Bar of Texas
1414 Colorado
PO Box 12487
Austin, TX 78711
(512) 463-1463

*http://www.texasbar.com/
start.htm*

UTAH

Utah State Bar
645 South 200 East, Suite 310
Salt Lake City, UT 84111
(801) 531-9077

http://www.utahbar.org

VERMONT

Vermont Bar Association
PO Box 100
Montpelier, VT 05601
(802) 223-2020

http://www.vtbar.org

VIRGINIA

Virginia State Bar
707 East Main Street, suite 1500
Richmond, VA 23219-0501
(804) 775-0500

Virginia Bar Association
701 East Franklin St., Suite 1120
Richmond, VA 23219
(804) 644-0041
http://www.vbar.org

VIRGIN ISLANDS

Virgin Islands Bar Association
P.O. Box 4108
Christiansted, Virgin Islands 00822
(340) 778-7497

WASHINGTON

Washington State Bar Association
500 Westin Street
2001 Sixth Avenue
Seattle, WA 98121-2599
(206) 727-8200
http://www.wsba.org

WEST VIRGINIA

West Virginia State Bar
2006 Kanawha Blvd. East
Charleston, WV 25311
(304) 558-2456
http://www.wvbar.org

West Virginia Bar Association
904 Security Building
100 Capitol Street
Charleston, WV 25301
(304) 342-1474

WISCONSIN

State Bar of Wisconsin
402 West Wilson Street
Madison, WI 53703
(608) 257-3838
*http://www.wisbar.org/
home.htm*

WYOMING

Wyoming State Bar
500 Randall Avenue
Cheyenne, WY 82001
PO Box 109
Cheyenne, WY 82003
(307) 632-9061
http://www.wyomingbar.org

Appendices

APPENDIX I

ALABAMA

Interstate Procedures	Same as intrastate procedures; guidelines information compiled and agreement sought; lacking agreement, evidence is presented to a court for a finding.
Income Considered for Setting Support	Wages, tips, commissions, bonuses, and other types of remuneration for services; unemployment compensation, workers' compensation not included in Alabama definitions
Criteria for Rebuttal	A written finding on record based on evidence the application of guidelines would be inappropriate, agreement establishing a different amount and stating the reasons therefore, then reviewed and approved by the court.
Support Order for Prior Periods	Yes; two years prior to filing of paternity action or back to the birth of the child if the child is less than two years old when action is commenced.
Jurisdiction Requirements	Yes
Modification Procedures	Petitions filed by agency upon request of either the client of an agency determination that action is appropriate following review of order.
Criteria for Modification	At the request of either party when order not reviewed or modified within 12 months unless undue hardship would result from inaction, and one party alleges a substantial change in circumstances; medical support has not been ordered.
Criteria for Change of Circumstances	A change which is substantial and continuing; primarily a change in needs of the child but also considers a change in parent ability to pay
Frequency of Reviews	Every 3 years or at request of either party to the order on non-assigned cases in accordance with state criteria.
Criteria for Review	Every 3 years or at request of either party
Criteria for Adjustment	Change in circumstances which is substantial and continuing

ALASKA

Interstate Procedures	Notice and Finding of Financial Responsibility served on obligor, who can request informal conference; support based on Alaska guidelines; appeals include formal hearing and judicial review.
Income Considered for Setting Support	Total income from all sources
Criteria for Rebuttal	Clear and convincing evidence
Support Order for Prior Periods	6 years prior to service of paternity complaint or administrative notice or non-AFDC service of complaint
Jurisdiction Requirements	CEJ analysis per UIFSA
Modification Procedures	CSED will, upon request in non-AFDC cases and every 3 years in AFDC cases, review child support orders for possible modification of the child support obligation and for medical support using current financial information. Reviews can be requested on either administrative or judicial orders.
Criteria for Modification	Substantial change in circumstances based on 15% or higher
Criteria for Change of Circumstances	15%
Frequency of Reviews	Every 3 years based on AFDC cases or upon the request of non-AFDC case party
Criteria for Review	Every 3 years based on AFDC cases or upon the request of non-AFDC case party
Criteria for Adjustment	Every 3 years based on AFDC cases or upon the request of non-AFDC case party

ARIZONA

Interstate Procedures	Upon receipt, case processed in same manner as a local case, using all procedures and techniques. Initiating jurisdiction must request "fair and equitable" support award for Arizona guidelines to apply
Income Considered for Setting Support	1) Special medical needs of the child, cost of providing health insurance for child, child care costs, custodial parent's gross income/assets; age of child; non-custodial parent's gross income/assets; second family. 2) Adjusted gross income of both parents
Criteria for Rebuttal	No
Support Order for Prior Periods	Post paternity cases: retroactive application of guidelines to the date of birth of child is used to direct amount defendant pays for past support. Marital cases: retroactive application of guidelines to date of filing dissolution of marriage the amount parents pay for past support of child.
Jurisdiction Requirements	None
Modification Procedures	1) "Simplified" requires filing court approved forms, notice to other party, request for hearing; "Standard" requires filing "Order to Show Cause" and "Comparative Spouse Affidavit", with hearing. 2) "Simplified" requires filing forms with court and forms served upon both parties; "Order to Show Cause" compels parties to a hearing regarding modification of existing order; "Conference" requires both parties to attend a conference to agree on new support amount.
Criteria for Modification	A variance of 15% or greater from current support order, continuing and substantial change in financial circumstances.
Criteria for Change of Circumstances	1) Modification of amount sought must minimally deviate at least 15% from existing order; 2) Financial circumstances must indicate the same and that substantial change in circumstance will be ongoing and for a period greater than 3 months.
Frequency of Reviews	Every 3 years; non-public assistance cases reviewed on per request basis, upon substantial continuing change in circumstances
Criteria for Review	Increase or decrease of 15% in current order, 3 years since last review, or substantial continuing change in financial circumstances of the payer.
Criteria for Adjustment	Lack of medical support provision; variance of 15% against current support order.

ARKANSAS

Interstate Procedures	UIFSA Provisions
Income Considered for Setting Support	Income as defined by federal income tax laws less deductions for federal and state income tax, FICA or railroad retirement, medical insurance for children, present paid child support for other dependents by court order.
Criteria for Rebuttal	Special medical or educational needs of child; cost of day care for child; non-custodial parent's net income/assets, self-support reserves; shared/joint custody arrangements; contributions to a trust fund for the child
Support Order for Prior Periods	Petition for retroactive support to the birth of the child in the initial action to establish paternity and support or to the date of the petition for support if paternity previously established.
Jurisdiction Requirements	UIFSA Provisions
Modification Procedures	UIFSA Provisions
Criteria for Modification	Continuous Exclusive Jurisdiction or consent of both parties
Criteria for Change of Circumstances	20% or $100 change per month in gross income
Frequency of Reviews	Once every 36 months from the date of the most recent order or review
Criteria for Review	All AFDC cases; non-AFDC cases upon request of either party
Criteria for Adjustment	Criteria for change of circumstances met and amount adjusted to meet guidelines

CALIFORNIA

Interstate Procedures	Complaint to establish filed with court. Non-custodial parent is served, with 30 days to respond. If no response, default taken. If answer filed, action set for trial.
Income Considered for Setting Support	Net monthly disposable income of each parent.
Criteria for Rebuttal	Support not assigned and parties stipulate to different amount; deferred sale/rental of home exceeds mortgage payments, insurance and taxes; paying parent has very high income; custodial time does not equal payment amount; unjust or inappropriate amount.
Support Order for Prior Periods	A support order may be made retroactive to the date of the filing the notice of motion or order to show cause. State law allows, in AFDC cases, support to be collected retroactively 3 years prior to the date the complaint was filed.
Jurisdiction Requirements	California must have continuing exclusive jurisdiction.
Modification Procedures	Orders can be modified upon a showing of substantial change of circumstances; Income and Expense Declarations must be filed by both parties; child support is calculated from declarations and based on non-custodial parent's ability to pay.
Criteria for Modification	At the request of either party if: guidelines indicate amount must increase or decrease by at least $50 or 30% whichever is greater, and change anticipated to last at least 6 months or medical insurance is available.
Criteria for Change of Circumstances	Increase or decrease in order of $50 or 30%, whichever is greater, or medical insurance becomes available.
Frequency of Reviews	Automatically reviewed every 36 months unless one party requests and: case was reviewed in last 12 months, modified within 24 months, quarterly locate unsuccessful.
Criteria for Review	See Frequency of Reviews
Criteria for Adjustment	See Criteria for Modification

COLORADO

Interstate Procedures	Processed same as in-state cases. Administrative process available for establishment of paternity and support.
Income Considered for Setting Support	Gross income from any source whatsoever, except child support payments received
Criteria for Rebuttal	Support order will be based on Colorado guidelines. Deviation from guidelines requires judicial intervention.
Support Order for Prior Periods	Yes
Jurisdiction Requirements	CEJ analysis per UIFSA
Modification Procedures	Modification may be for either increases or decreases in child or medical support obligation. Colorado uses current income information and state statute requirements to review the case. Child support orders may be adjusted based upon a 10% change in child support calculation or for inclusion of medical support, which constitute a continuing change in circumstances.
Criteria for Modification	Change up or down of at least 10%; total support change; no dollar requirement if review and adjustment is just to add medical insurance requirement.
Criteria for Change of Circumstances	Definition of "substantial change of circumstance" is a 10% variance in guideline calculation
Frequency of Reviews	Every 3 years or upon request of either party
Criteria for Review	(For both) Order at least 36 months old; IV-D or medical support case; AFDC, medical assistance only; IV-E foster care without written request; no assistance or state-funded FC; exception to 36 months rule with demonstrated 10% change.
Criteria for Adjustment	

CONNECTICUT

Interstate Procedures	URESA petitions sent to central registry. Support enforcement division dockets case in family support magistrate division of superior court, sets hearing and issues summons.
Income Considered for Setting Support	Net income of both parents; net income includes all gross income except other child support received and federal, state or local public assistance grants; taxes, insurance premiums, union dues/fees, alimony and child support for outside party are deductible.
Criteria for Rebuttal	Other financial resources available to parent; extraordinary expenses for child or parent; needs of parent's other dependents; special circumstances outlined in §46b-215a-3 of Connecticut State Agencies .
Support Order for Prior Periods	Yes (3 year limit for paternity cases)
Jurisdiction Requirements	URESA
Modification Procedures	Direct interstate referral form requesting review and adjustment of order to local Support Enforcement Division office. Support Enforcement Division will prepare appropriate motions if jurisdiction can be obtained, and notify requesting jurisdiction of results.
Criteria for Modification	Substantial change in circumstances of either party or deviation of existing support order from child support guidelines amount (at least 15% deviation).
Criteria for Change of Circumstances	Child emancipated or changed household residence; modification of orders after paternity adjudication, or birth of child after dissolution of marriage; an arrearage order exists; child resides with different custodial relatives; changes to ensure proper collection.
Frequency of Reviews	Every 3 years in AFDC or foster care cases; in all others, upon request of IV-D agency, either parent or guardian
Criteria for Review	AFDC/foster care cases: 36 months since last order or review, without case closure criteria met, good cause granted, not in child's best interest or neither parent requested review. Non-AFDC cases: Significant deviation of 15% in income/assets or more from child support guidelines or written request for review.
Criteria for Adjustment	See Criteria for Modification

DELAWARE

Interstate Procedures	Yes
Income Considered for Setting Support	Gross income/assets of both parties; second family involvement; inflationary factors
Criteria for Rebuttal	The Delaware "Melson" formula is rebuttable only by a finding on the record that an order established pursuant to the guidelines would be unjust or inappropriate.
Support Order for Prior Periods	Maximum two years, at discretion of Court.
Jurisdiction Requirements	Delaware has personal jurisdiction or party submits to Delaware's jurisdiction by consent.
Modification Procedures	Register order in Delaware and file petition for modification, specifying grounds.
Criteria for Modification	Age of order
Criteria for Change of Circumstances	Medical expenses; income change of either party
Frequency of Reviews	Order is at least 2 1/2 years old, unless a substantial change in circumstances was brought on by no fault of the petitioner.
Criteria for Review	
Criteria for Adjustment	

DISTRICT OF COLUMBIA

Interstate Procedures	Upon receipt, case assigned and referred to Superior Court; Office of the Corporation Counsel handles IV-D legal representation on behalf of petitioner; D.C. guidelines apply; stipulations for support used but legal establishment of support requires court order
Income Considered for Setting Support	Cost of providing health insurance for child; child care costs; custodial parent's gross income/assets; age of child; non-custodial parent's gross income/assets; second family involvement; number of children
Criteria for Rebuttal	Needs of child are exceptional; non-custodial parent's gross income substantially less than custodial parent; other support obligations; non-custodial parent requires debt reduction for not more than 12 months; any other exceptional circumstances.
Support Order for Prior Periods	Birth of child plus pre-natal expenses, requiring proof of income from both parties, proof of child care expenses and proof of medical insurance cost for the relevant period.
Jurisdiction Requirements	CEJ analysis per UIFSA
Modification Procedures	Request from initiating state for modification/increase with Motion to Increase affidavit from initiating state; motion filed in Superior Court, summons issued, service on obligor, hearing held, determination made, and order entered.
Criteria for Modification	The application of the guidelines against the current child support order must result in an award that varies by 15% or more change from the existing child support order.
Criteria for Change of Circumstances	No modifications in support obligation in past three years; change in needs of the child or the ability of a parent to provide support.
Frequency of Reviews	Upon request of any party; status request; birth of a new child or every three years.
Criteria for Review	Upon request
Criteria for Adjustment	Adjustment must be at least a 15% variation from existing child support order.

FLORIDA

Interstate Procedures	Judicial
Income Considered for Setting Support	Income of legal parents is factored; any form of payment to non-custodial parent regardless of the source.
Criteria for Rebuttal	Judge may deviate 5% without stating a reason; deviation above 5% requires court record to contain written finding stating why application of guidelines is inappropriate.
Support Order for Prior Periods	Yes, depending on jurisdiction and case specific information. Prior period may begin at birth of child, date of separation, and/or date of filing case with the court. Criteria depends on jurisdictional requirements.
Jurisdiction Requirements	Modification only if permissible under Full Faith and Credit for Child Support Orders Act.
Modification Procedures	Review of child and medical support upon request of either parent; AFDC, Title IV-E Foster Care and Non-AFDC Medicaid cases reviewed every 3 years. When a support order is inconsistent with the guideline amount by 15% or $50, whichever is greater, the modification process in enacted.
Criteria for Modification	If permissible, a change of 15% or $50, whichever is greater, based on criteria for change in circumstances.
Criteria for Change of Circumstances	Parent or child permanently disabled, has chronic illness, special and/or recurring medical needs, financial needs of child or income of either parent have changed significantly. Upon request of either parent; every 3 years in AFDC, Title IV-E and non-AFDC Medicaid cases.
Frequency of Reviews	Section 61.30, Florida statutes to include Criteria for Modification
Criteria for Review	See Criteria for Modification and Criteria for Change of Circumstances
Criteria for Adjustment	

GEORGIA

Interstate Procedures	alf no prior order exists, order must be established through URESA process and/or administrative process; if paternity is disputed, order must be established through URESA process
Income Considered for Setting Support	Non-custodial and custodial parents' incomes
Criteria for Rebuttal	None
Support Order for Prior Periods	No
Jurisdiction Requirements	Final actions filed in the county of the adversely affected party
Modification Procedures	In all AFDC cases and with written request in non-AFDC cases, orders are reviewed within 36 months after date of order. CSE reviews orders for modification of current support, medical support, and arrears/repay amount. The CSE Recommendation for Modification is submitted either to an Adminstrative Law Judge for Adminstrative Orders or the Superior Court for Judicial Orders with a request that an Order be issued adjusting the child support award.
Criteria for Modification	A determination that there is a significant inconsistency between the existing child support order and the amount resulting from the application of State codes.
Criteria for Change of Circumstances	Change of circumstances is not a criteria for modification.
Frequency of Reviews	Every three years
Criteria for Review	Medicaid with order at least 36 months old, with a written request.
Criteria for Adjustment	Modification must result in an increase or decrease by 15% or greater with minimum $25 per month increase or decrease

HAWAII

Interstate Procedures	Most cases handled by adminstrative process; no distinction between intrastate and interstate cases
Income Considered for Setting Support	Non-custodial and custodial parents' gross incomes/assets.
Criteria for Rebuttal	Showing of exceptional circumstances
Support Order for Prior Periods	Yes, from birth of child and paternity actions; can go back to prior periods only for AFDC cases; discretionary with court hearings officer as to amount recoverable.
Jurisdiction Requirements	URESA
Modification Procedures	Non-AFDC cases: review by request of either parent. AFDC cases: review every 36 months from date of last order or by request. Upon notice of review, both parents have thirty days to provide updated financial information before review initiated. If neither party requests a hearing, an administrative order is signed and filed with the Family Court. If a hearing is requested, an order is entered based on the results of the hearing.
Criteria for Modification	Every three years in AFDC cases; a change in circumstances; statutes require a change in child support guidelines
Criteria for Change of Circumstances	Must be substantial and material change in either of the parents' or child's circumstances
Frequency of Reviews	Upon request of either parent or guardian, and upon receipt of information that there is a change in circumstances warranting a modification.
Criteria for Review	Upon request of either parent or guardian, and upon receipt of information that there is a change in circumstances warranting a modification.
Criteria for Adjustment	Changes of more than $10

IDAHO

Interstate Procedures	Judicial Process Only. UIFSA
Income Considered for Setting Support	All sources of income. Rarely is the income of the current spouse required.
Criteria for Rebuttal	Idaho Rules of Civil procedure 6(c)(6) Child Support Guidelines require the court to make a specific finding that application of guidelines is inappropriate in a particular case.
Support Order for Prior Periods	Yes, limited to the 36 months preceding the date of filing in court.
Jurisdiction Requirements	UIFSA: Model Act provisions; non-UIFSA: Idaho orders, retained jurisdiction.
Modification Procedures	Administrative reviews conducted every three years. In non-AFDC cases, proceeding requires a request by one of the parties, notice of intent to review and request for information, notice of findings, amended notice of findings if applicable, judicial proceedings to modify.
Criteria for Modification	Substantial and material change in circumstances required.
Criteria for Change of Circumstances	The change must be substantial and material, such as change in custody or extraordinary medical expenses. Unemployment, voluntary unemployment, or under-employment is considered temporary and will not qualify as substantial change.
Frequency of Reviews	36 months unless a substantial and material change in circumstance occurs sooner
Criteria for Review	Every 36 months, a claim of substantial and material change in circumstances, or an increase or decrease of at least $50 per month.
Criteria for Adjustment	An increase or decrease of at least $50 or 15% per month of the amount of support.

ILLINOIS

Interstate Procedures	Referrals to establish support through adminstrative process require the following factual circumstances: Child was born or conceived during marriage, or after child's birth, support sought from man named as child's father on Illinois birth certificate, or in matters involving alleged paternity with support sought by either child's mother or alleged father.
Income Considered for Setting Support	750 ILCS 5/505, non-custodial parent's net income/assets (percentage related to number of children)
Criteria for Rebuttal	Child's prior status of living, and assets of child, custodial parent and non-custodial parent
Support Order for Prior Periods	Legislation supporting action passed, policy being written
Jurisdiction Requirements	In accordance with UIFSA
Modification Procedures	In accordance with UIFSA. Review processes under federal regulations and modification pursuant to UIFSA.
Criteria for Modification	If order is at least three years old, it can be modified showing a 20% or more change under the guidelines, otherwise substantial change in circumstances must be shown.
Criteria for Change of Circumstances	For increase: a) concrete change in needs of child must be shown; b) financial resources and needs of custodial parent are considered, income of current spouse being relevant; or c) financial resources and needs of non-custodial parent are considered, income of current spouse being relevant. For decrease: proof of reduced need by child or reduced ability to pay support by non-custodial parent.
Frequency of Reviews	Every three years on IV-A cases; as requested on non-assistance cases.
Criteria for Review	20% change in support compared to the guidelines (minimum $10 per month)
Criteria for Adjustment	20% change in support compared to the guidelines (minimum $10 per month)

INDIANA

Interstate Procedures	
Income Considered for Setting Support	
Criteria for Rebuttal	
Support Order for Prior Periods	May only do so in paternity cases
Jurisdiction Requirements	Follows UIFSA
Modification Procedures	
Criteria for Modification	
Criteria for Change of Circumstances	
Frequency of Reviews	
Criteria for Review	Substantial change in circumstances
Criteria for Adjustment	Per guidelines, a change of 20% or more from current order

IOWA

Interstate Procedures	Standard URESA referral. If paternity is not an issue, adminstrative order for support is entered unless there is an existing order for current support.
Income Considered for Setting Support	Net monthly incomes of both custodial and non-custodial parents.
Criteria for Rebuttal	Adjustments are necessary to provide for needs of the child and do justice between the parties under special circumstances of case; circumstances associated with permanency and hardship plan for children in foster care.
Support Order for Prior Periods	Yes, up to three years of AFDC expenditures, arrearages not sought for NPA cases
Jurisdiction Requirements	Iowa or foreign order in accordance with federal Full Faith and Credit for Child Support Orders Act 28USC, 1738B
Modification Procedures	Petition filed in district court or adminstrative modification available as part of review and adjust process.
Criteria for Modification	Substantial change in circumstances or inconsistency with child support guidelines
Criteria for Change of Circumstances	10% variation from guidelines represents a "substantial change in circumstances"; 20% variation needed to initiate modification procedure; CSE agency may also modify an order solely to include medical support.
Frequency of Reviews	Two years from order or last modification when requested; every three years when initiated by IV-D agency for public assistance cases.
Criteria for Review	IV-D case, parent's location known; Iowa or foreign order; meets review requirements; request by parent/agency entitled to such; lasting change in financial circumstances
Criteria for Adjustment	Present child support obligation varies more than 20% from guidelines; availability of health insurance

KANSAS

Interstate Procedures	URESA/UIFSA pleadings required; Central Registry initiates procedures; attorneys generally seek order based on guidelines; copy of order sent to initiating state.
Income Considered for Setting Support	Non-custodial parent's income from all sources, excluding public assistance. Includes any income which is regularly/periodically received from any source.
Criteria for Rebuttal	Calculation of respective parental child support obligations is a rebuttable presumption of a reasonable child support order. Court completes Section E of Child Support Worksheet listing all relevant child support adjustments.
Support Order for Prior Periods	Yes, limited to the 36 months preceding the date of filing in court.
Jurisdiction Requirements	CEJ analysis per UIFSA
Modification Procedures	Central Registry initiates procedures; if modification of another state's order is sought, the order must first be registered; for modification of Kansas order, attorney files motion to modify; if a hearing is needed, court determines if there has been a change based on guidelines and adjustments allowed if in child's best interests. A Kansas support order is automatically reduced by child's pro rata share when child is emancipated, dies, is adopted, or lives permanently with obligor.
Criteria for Modification	Review for child support on a three year cycle, upon request in non-assistance cases and without request in AFDC cases; modification upon material change in circumstances
Criteria for Change of Circumstances	Material change in circumstances includes: 10% or more change in non-custodial parent's finances; 7th and 16th birthdays of child; emancipation of child; failure to comply with court award obligations; group health insurance now available; change in custody.
Frequency of Reviews	Every three years (AFDC cases); upon request of either party, once every two years.
Criteria for Review	
Criteria for Adjustment	See Criteria for Modification and Criteria for Change of Circumstances

KENTUCKY

Interstate Procedures	Administrative or Judicial
Income Considered for Setting Support	Commissions, earnings, salaries, wages, and income due or to be due in future from employer and successors, profit sharing plan, pension plan, insurance contract, annuity, social security, lottery winnings, unemployment compensation, workers' compensation
Criteria for Rebuttal	Yes
Support Order for Prior Periods	Yes
Jurisdiction Requirements	URESA
Modification Procedures	Must register other state's order
Criteria for Modification	Kentucky order; order 36 months old; child must not become emancipated within the next 18 months
Criteria for Change of Circumstances	15% change in obligation
Frequency of Reviews	Every 3 years, or upon request of either party
Criteria for Review	Every 3 years, or upon request of either party
Criteria for Adjustment	Kentucky order; order 36 months old; child must not become emancipated within the next 18 months

LOUISIANA

Interstate Procedures	After receipt and filing of petition from the initiating state, an order is established according to Louisiana law and guidelines.
Income Considered for Setting Support	Gross incomes of both non-custodial and custodial parents. Income of a child may also be considered.
Criteria for Rebuttal	Only the court may deviate from the guidelines.
Support Order for Prior Periods	Order entered retroactive to the date of filing of the petition.
Jurisdiction Requirements	CEJ analysis per UIFSA
Modification Procedures	Register order; file a petition for modification after due notices to parties involved.
Criteria for Modification	None for medical support. At least 25% change in the obligation amount.
Criteria for Change of Circumstances	Needs of the child and parent's ability to pay, and changes relative to one or both of these factors.
Frequency of Reviews	Every three years (AFDC and IV-E cases); upon request of either parent.
Criteria for Review	Needs of the child and parent's ability to pay, and changes relative to one or both of these factors.
Criteria for Adjustment	None for medical support. At least 25% change in the obligation amount.

MAINE

Interstate Procedures	Current support and debts for past support established administratively pursuant to Alternative Method of Support Enforcement (19 MSRA §§491-516).
Income Considered for Setting Support	Wages, salary, commissions, bonuses, pension and retirement program payments, insurance policies, gain from capital and/or labor, profit through sale or conversion of capital assets, unemployment compensation and workers' compensation benefits.
Criteria for Rebuttal	Finding that guidelines-based award would be inequitable, unjust, or inappropriate, or not in child's best interest (see MRSA §317 (3)).
Support Order for Prior Periods	Yes, up to six years prior to commencement of an action to establish an order for past support. Documents required include: affidavit as to gross income/work-related day-care expenses of custodial parent; income/asset forms required by Rules of Maine Supreme Court; affidavit of past payment/nonpayment.
Jurisdiction Requirements	UIFSA, 19 MSRA § 426-J
Modification Procedures	Motion for amendment for Maine court orders; modification only if evidence of more than 15% deviation from Maine guidelines; older orders and reviews previously requested take precedence.
Criteria for Modification	Substantial change of circumstances; by statute, deviation of more than 15% from Maine's guidelines.
Criteria for Change of Circumstances	Deviation of more than 15% from Maine's guidelines.
Frequency of Reviews	Every three years, resources permitting.
Criteria for Review	Deviation more than 15% from Maine guidelines; whether non-custodial parent can obtain or maintain health insurance coverage at a reasonable cost.
Criteria for Adjustment	Deviation more than 15% from Maine guidelines; whether non-custodial parent can obtain or maintain health insurance coverage at a reasonable cost.

MARYLAND

Interstate Procedures	Judicial process; send URESA petition with Transmittal FSA-200, ICR reviews and send to local court; State's attorney gets consent from obligor or prosecutes case.
Income Considered for Setting Support	Gross income from commissions, salaries, wages, bonuses; dividend, pension, interest, trust, and annuity incomes; Social Security, workers' compensation, unemployment, and disability insurance benefits; alimony or maintenance received.
Criteria for Rebuttal	Second intact family; prior agreement between parties.
Support Order for Prior Periods	Yes, if for child other than child for whom support is sought.
Jurisdiction Requirements	
Modification Procedures	3 certified copies of URESA petition and document change in circumstance
Criteria for Modification	25% change in support obligated amount
Criteria for Change of Circumstances	If application of guidelines would produce a 25% change in support obligated amount, or at the discretion of the court upon showing a material change in circumstance.
Frequency of Reviews	Every three years for AFDC cases, otherwise when either party has requested a review with 36 months since the last order or review.
Criteria for Review	For AFDC, if it is 36 months since the last order or review; non-AFDC when either party has requested a review and it is 36 months since the last order or review.
Criteria for Adjustment	Application of guidelines would produce at least 25% change in support amount

MASSACHUSETTS

Interstate Procedures	UIFSA, judicial procedures for establishment
Income Considered for Setting Support	Gross income
Criteria for Rebuttal	Obligor has other children whom he is legally required to support
Support Order for Prior Periods	Yes. Depending upon the circumstances of the case, may go as far back as pre-natal period.
Jurisdiction Requirements	UIFSA
Modification Procedures	DOR staff review case, pursue adjustment in court if appropriate
Criteria for Modification	Change in order upon application of guidelines and need for health coverage
Criteria for Change of Circumstances	N/A
Frequency of Reviews	Every 3 years, or upon request
Criteria for Review	Every 3 years, or upon request
Criteria for Adjustment	Change in order upon application of guidelines and need for health coverage

MICHIGAN

Interstate Procedures	1) URESA petitions handled by Prosecuting Attorney in respondent's county; 2) URESA registration requests handled by Friend of the Court in obligor's county; 3) Interstate Income Withholding requests processed by Friend of the Court in county of obligor's employer; 4) Support collections processed by Friend of the Court where order entered.
Income Considered for Setting Support	Cost of child's health insurance, child care costs, net income/assets of both parents, second family involvement, inflationary factors, custodial arrangements, pre-existing orders, visitation abatement.
Criteria for Rebuttal	Applying guidelines would be unfair and unjust.
Support Order for Prior Periods	Paternity Act authorizes support for prior periods, provided filing occurs before age six.
Jurisdiction Requirements	Orders registered in Michigan fall under jurisdiction of circuit courts.
Modification Procedures	Friend of the Court must review child support orders not less than once every 2 years when: • A party requests a review in writing • Child subject to the order received AFDC or Medicaid unless good cause exists not to proceed with support action or the order provides for health care coverage, and neither party requested a review. • The initiating state requests a review on behalf of a Title IV-D services recipient.
Criteria for Modification	Criteria includes a change in physical custody of child not court ordered, increased or decreased needs of a child; changed financial conditions of parties, probable access by an employed parent to dependent health care coverage.
Criteria for Change of Circumstances	N/A
Frequency of Reviews	See Criteria for Modification
Criteria for Review	Every 24 months as described in procedures.
Criteria for Adjustment	10% of ordered amount, or 5% per week, whichever is less.

MINNESOTA

Interstate Procedures	Administrative process if case is a consent or default; if case is contested, it could become judicial. Adm. Process Statute 518.5511
Income Considered for Setting Support	Non-custodial parent's net income/assets, periodic income, salary, wages, commissions, deferred compensation, certain overtime, dividends, interest, trust income, and work-related benefits, compensation and bonuses; spousal maintenance received, disability benefits. Also number of children, child care costs and costs of child's health insurance.
Criteria for Rebuttal	See Mn. Stat. 518.551
Support Order for Prior Periods	Minnesota law allows reimbursement up to two years prior to the date action was started. Information has to be stated in the facts and order as to what amount of reimbursement you are asking for and how you arrived at the amount.
Jurisdiction Requirements	CEJ per UIFSA
Modification Procedures	Upon signed request for non-public assistance cases and automatically for public assistance cases, every 36 months. Workers may elect to do more as often as circumstances allow. Interstate requests for review must include a signature from a party or a IV-D worker and sufficient financial information to review.
Criteria for Modification	Difference of 20% and a minimum of $50 higher or lower with application of Minnesota guidelines than the current order. If due to change in circumstances, must be a change longer than 6 months. Fluctuations in child care must meet the dollar standard.
Criteria for Change of Circumstances	Failure to comply with medical support provisions and at least 20% and minimum of $50 change up or down.
Frequency of Reviews	Every 3 years at minimum.
Criteria for Review	Order at least 35 months old; IV-D or medical support enforcement case; AFDC, MA or IV-E Foster care without request, or non-public assistance with request; UIFSA CEJ requirements must be met.
Criteria for Adjustment	See Criteria for Modification; Minnesota has biannual cost of living increase (COLA).

MISSISSIPPI

Interstate Procedures	URESA; Interstate income withholding
Income Considered for Setting Support	Extraordinary medical, psychological, educational, or dental expenses; independent income of child; payment of both child support and spousal support to obligee; seasonal variations in one or both parents' income or expenses; age of the child; special needs; time spent with non-custodial parent; total available assets of both parents and child.
Criteria for Rebuttal	N/A
Support Order for Prior Periods	N/A
Jurisdiction Requirements	N/A
Modification Procedures	IV-D cases with assignments to the state are reviewed every three years or sooner if requested by either parent. A review must be requested by the other state or either parent in cases without assignments to the state.
Criteria for Modification	15% change in adjusted income of either parent, or change in the needs of the child
Criteria for Change of Circumstances	Extraordinary medical expenses, independent income of the child, available assets of the child, age of the child, change in involvement of non-custodial parent in child's activities
Frequency of Reviews	Every 3 years, or upon request
Criteria for Review	15% change in adjusted income of either parent, or change in the needs of the child
Criteria for Adjustment	15% change in adjusted income of either parent, or change in the needs of the child

MISSOURI

Interstate Procedures	Handled same as local cases; Missouri enforces existing order. If no order, established through administrative process. URESA process in circuit court when paternity is contested; requesting state must require order for genetic testing and necessaries.
Income Considered for Setting Support	Custodial parent's gross income/assets; non-custodial parent's gross income/assets; other child and spousal support being paid. Income may be imputed for unemployed and underemployed parents as well as in cases in which current income is unknown.
Criteria for Rebuttal	Court or administrative agency enters a written or specific finding on the record that the presumed amount is unjust or inappropriate.
Support Order for Prior Periods	Yes; request should indicate period for which support is sought, financial income information for the period, and AFDC paid out during the period. Period limited to five years preceding the commencement of the action in paternity cases. Only pursued by county prosecutors; no administrative establishment procedures.
Jurisdiction Requirements	Follow CEJ requirements in Full Faith and Credit for Child Support Orders Act. If Missouri is to modify, order is registered under Section 454.340, RSMo then modified.
Modification Procedures	Upon request in AFDC cases and with or without a request in AFDC cases, orders are reviewed every three years for child support and medical support modification, for increase or decrease in support. Financial information on both parties is obtained. Modified through Missouri administrative orders of judicial orders through administrative process. Parties have the right to request administrative hearing to contest the motion to modify. When a judicial order is modified administratively, modified order is sent to court for approval. The court has 45 days to approve order or set it for trial. DCSE can refer modification case to attorney or contract attorney to file a petition with the court to have the order modified.
Criteria for Modification	Presumed child support differs 20% or more (higher or lower) than present obligation; child ceases to meet requirements to receive current support and other child are on order; health insurance obligation needs to be added to order.
Criteria for Change of Circumstances	Changed circumstances so substantial and continuing as to make terms of order unreasonable; court considers financial resources of both parties, earning capacity of em-ployed parent, and if application of guidelines would alter current order by 20% or more
Frequency of Reviews	Every 3 years
Criteria for Review	Must be IV-D and order entered, modified or reviewed at least 36 months ago; AFDC, medical assistance only, or IV-E foster care done with or without a request; non-AFDC must have request; child ceases to meet requirements and other children remain on order; order lacks health insurance provision; alleged lasting 50% change in income.
Criteria for Adjustment	See Criteria for Modification

MONTANA

Interstate Procedures	Administrative process; handled same as state cases. In absence of support order, Notice of Financial Responsibility is served, default if no request for hearing, abstracted to District Court, use of mandatory support guidelines.
Income Considered for Setting Support	Gross/net income of both parents. Income received from all sources. Self-employement includes gross receipts minus ordinary and necessary expenses for operating business or self-employment. Also considered are special medical needs of child, health insurance for child, age of child, household size of both mother and father.
Criteria for Rebuttal	Evidence child's needs are not being met; showing application of guidelines would be unfair for child or one of the parties; the best interests of child. If order not based on support guidelines, Administrative Law Judge must include in order why guidelines are inappropriate. See MCA §40-5-226(5).
Support Order for Prior Periods	No. Obligation commences on first day of month immediately following month in which notice was issued.
Jurisdiction Requirements	CEJ analysis per UIFSA and subject matter and personal jurisdiction over necessary parties under MCA §40-5-272.
Modification Procedures	Administrative and court orders of other states reviewed only if subject matter jurisdiction obtained under UIFSA and personal jurisdiction over all parties. Administrative process used for modifying support and health insurance orders. First stage: preliminary guidelines computation performed; if parties are in agreement, a Modification Consent Order is prepared and signed; failure to respond is deemed to be consent to Order. Second stage: request for arbitration by either party and pre-hearing settlement telephone conference; should parties fail to reach agreement, Notice of Proposed Modification issued and parties have 30 days to challenge decision; failure to challenge results in final administrative order. Third stage: if administrative order challenged, hearing may be requested. At hearing's conclusion, an order representing the final decision in entered.
Criteria for Modification	Amount of monthly child support obligation in current order does not conform to guidelines; current order does not contain health insurance; current order does not provide credit for social security benefits due to obligor's disability.
Criteria for Change of Circumstances	Net income of either parent changes 25% or more; household composition of either parent has changed; change in custody/visitation; one or more children emancipated, at age of majority or child; new child born after order; obligor disabled; one or more children developed special needs or needs no longer exist; order set without using guidelines.
Frequency of Reviews	AFDC every 36 months; non-AFDC upon request 30 months after last order or review and significant change in circumstances has occurred.
Criteria for Review	AFDC every 36 months; non-AFDC upon request 30 months after last order or review and significant change in circumstances has occurred.
Criteria for Adjustment	Obligation increases/decreases $25 or more; modified order requires health insurance for child and/or provides for social security benefits for child due to obligor's disability.

NEBRASKA

Interstate Procedures	Judicial; UIFSA applies
Income Considered for Setting Support	Gross income of both parents; deductions for other child support obligor must pay, taxes, mandatory retirement payments, and union dues.
Criteria for Rebuttal	Extraordinary medical expenses for either parent or child; special needs of disabled child; juveniles placed in foster care; whenever application of guidelines would be unjust or inappropriate.
Support Order for Prior Periods	N/A
Jurisdiction Requirements	Nebraska must obtain continuing, exclusive jurisdiction; UIFSA exception regarding modification of registered foreign order.
Modification Procedures	Judicial process involving motion to modify, service of process, answer, hearing, and order; modification retroactive only back to date of service of motion to modify.
Criteria for Modification	Case is IV-D; modification of child support or medical coverage only; current order is at least 3 years old and it has been 3 years since last review; it is a current order and not for income withholding only, it is an active Nebraska order, and is not a tribal order; obligor is not institutionalized or incarcerated; at least one parent resides in Nebraska; last child in order will not be emancipated for another 12 months; financial circumstances have lasted 6 months and will last at least another 6 months.
Criteria for Change of Circumstances	Material change in circumstances; each case evaluated on its own merits for good cause shown; rebuttable presumption of material change created by 10% variation from current amount if changed circumstances have lasted 6 months and will last at least 3 more.
Frequency of Reviews	Upon request of either parent, or a guardian, but not more than once every 3 years.
Criteria for Review	Sufficient data to convince court a material change in circumstances exists/occurred.
Criteria for Adjustment	Sufficient data to convince court a material change in circumstances exists/occurred.

NEVADA

Interstate Procedures	Use of state guidelines to establish support amount based on non-custodial parent's gross income; establish immediate income withholding; non-custodial parent must provide health insurance if available at reasonable cost.
Income Considered for Setting Support	Non-custodial parent's gross income/assets
Criteria for Rebuttal	Cost of health insurance, child care; special educational needs of child; age of child; responsibility of parents for support of others; value of services contributed by both parents; public assistance; mother's pregnancy/confinement costs; travel expenses if custodial parent moves from original jurisdiction; time spent with child; other expenses for child.
Support Order for Prior Periods	Based on circumstances, may go back four years
Jurisdiction Requirements	URESA (NRS 130)
Modification Procedures	Upon request in non-assistance cases and without request in AFDC cases, every 3 years. One (1) year before modification or change.
Criteria for Modification	Order being enforced in Nevada; order is at least 3 years old; requests by either parent or guardian or IV-D agency. Application of state guidelines warrants 15% increase or decrease in support order and/or availability of health insurance.
Criteria for Change of Circumstances	At least 20% change with minimum $75 increase/decrease in non-custodial parent's obligation; must be at least one year from last order or review. Also any case when custodial parent wants to cover child's health insurance or non-custodial parent's employment does not cover child with health insurance
Frequency of Reviews	Every three years; upon request of either parent or guardian for non-AFDC cases, or upon request of interstate IV-D agency for out-of-state AFDC cases.
Criteria for Review	Order at least 35 months old
Criteria for Adjustment	See Criteria for Modification

NEW HAMPSHIRE

Interstate Procedures	OCS submits a recommended order to the court for Judge's signature.
Income Considered for Setting Support	Gross income from any source minus support paid under court or administrative order, 50% of amount paid for health insurance for child(ren), mandatory contributions to retirement plans and actual state income taxes paid, and day care expenses.
Criteria for Rebuttal	A written or specific finding that application of guidelines would be unjust or inappropriate as determined using state's criteria.
Support Order for Prior Periods	Yes, 6 years for AFDC cases, no limit for other types.
Jurisdiction Requirements	New Hampshire order, must get personal service/jurisdiction under Full Faith and Credit
Modification Procedures	Interstate Enforcement transmittal and notarized financial statement from custodial parent
Criteria for Modification	Substantial change in circumstances or three years since last order. IV-D agency reviews only if a 20% change and at least $50 per month change; no medical support included in original order
Criteria for Change of Circumstances	Change must be permanent, involuntary, and substantial.
Frequency of Reviews	Not more than every 3 years for AFDC cases or upon request for non-AFDC cases; must show change in financial circumstances in non-AFDC cases
Criteria for Review	Compliance with guidelines
Criteria for Adjustment	See Criteria for Modification

NEW JERSEY

Interstate Procedures	Expedited processes; petition is received at central registry and processed; notice sent to non-custodial parent; if consent is not reached, case is scheduled for a hearing.
Income Considered for Setting Support	Gross income/assets of both parents; second family involvement; child support and/or alimony orders from other relationship.
Criteria for Rebuttal	A written or specific finding on the record stating that the amount is unjust or inappropriate.
Support Order for Prior Periods	N/A
Jurisdiction Requirements	N/A
Modification Procedures	Formal motion is filed with the court.
Criteria for Modification	There must be a 20% change from the existing order.
Criteria for Change of Circumstances	Change in circumstance is continuing; agreement or decree has made explicit provision for change; increase in need of custodial parent compared to original order; decrease in amount if not needed; modification also based upon non-custodial parent's ability to pay.
Frequency of Reviews	Every three years for AFDC cases; upon request of either parent, or a guardian, in non-AFDC cases
Criteria for Review	Every three years for AFDC cases; upon request of either parent, or a guardian, in non-AFDC cases
Criteria for Adjustment	A 20% change from the existing order.

NEW MEXICO

Interstate Procedures	UIFSA adopted verbatim
Income Considered for Setting Support	Actual gross income of parent, from any and all sources, if parent is employed to full capacity, or potential income if unemployed or underemployed. Gross income does not include income of subsequent spouses.
Criteria for Rebuttal	A finding that application of guidelines would be unjust or inappropriate, or which may include a substantial hardship on any party.
Support Order for Prior Periods	Yes. Support retroactive to date of child's birth. May direct father to pay reasonable expenses of mother's pregnancy, birth, and confinement.
Jurisdiction Requirements	UIFSA
Modification Procedures	Automatic review every 3 years. Financial affidavits/information obtained to complete review; parties notified of review in writing. If review indicates modification, both parties are given 30 days to respond to finding. Right to seek modification rests with the department in cases with assignment of support rights.
Criteria for Modification	Application of current guidelines would result in 20% or more deviation from existing order, and petition for modification filed more than one year after filing of existing order.
Criteria for Change of Circumstances	Not defined in statute.
Frequency of Reviews	At least every three years in AFDC cases; at either party's request in non-AFDC cases.
Criteria for Review	See above.
Criteria for Adjustment	See above.

NEW YORK

Interstate Procedures	Hearing conducted whereupon respondent may request amount based on guidelines or oppose amount; case matter postponed for hearing examiner to review facts and determine support amount.
Income Considered for Setting Support	Income includes gross total income as should be or have been reported on the most recent federal income tax return and may also include: investment income, benefits not included, attributed income from available sources, self-employment deductions.
Criteria for Rebuttal	10 factors including: financial resources of parents and child; physical and emotional health of child; child's special needs; child's previous standard of living; tax consequences to parties; non-monetary contributions to child's care; educational needs of parents; substantial difference in parents' incomes; extraordinary expenses incurred exercising visitation rights; any other factors deemed relevant by the court.
Support Order for Prior Periods	Orders are effective from either date petition is filed, or date public assistance granted; support may be ordered retroactive to birth of child at court's discretion.
Jurisdiction Requirements	Orders issued by New York courts but not registered orders
Modification Procedures	File petition with court alleging change of circumstances.
Criteria for Modification	A significant and unforseen change of circumstances with regard to various factors.
Criteria for Change of Circumstances	A significant and unforseen change of circumstances with regard to various factors.
Frequency of Reviews	If AFDC, IV-E, MA: only once every three years; if non-AFDC, once every three years upon request of either party.
Criteria for Review	If AFDC, IV-E, MA: only once every three years; if non-AFDC, once every three years upon request of either party.
Criteria for Adjustment	If calculated order amount differs 10% or more than reviewed order, or if order does not have provision for health care coverage.

NORTH CAROLINA

Interstate Procedures	UIFSA; local IV-D contacts defendant for voluntary support agreement; documents reviewed by district court judge who signs order approving support agreement; if defendant not willing to enter support agreement, case is scheduled for court.
Income Considered for Setting Support	Gross income from any source, including but not limited to: wages, salaries, commissions, bonuses, dividends, severance pay, pensions, interest, trust income, annuities, capital gains, social security, workers' compensation, disability, insurance and unemployment benefits, gifts, prizes, and alimony/maintenance from other parties.
Criteria for Rebuttal	Guidelines are rebuttable; guidelines amount mandatory unless basis for deviation would be inequitable to either party.
Support Order for Prior Periods	Yes; 3 year limit on claim from date expenditure was made.
Jurisdiction Requirements	North Carolina must have CEJ under UIFSA
Modification Procedures	A court order is modified upon motion in the cause and showing of substantial changed circumstance affecting the welfare of child by either parent or interested party.
Criteria for Modification	A 15% change in amount between existing order and amount based on guidelines, and if existing order is at least 3 years old. If less than 3 years old, party requesting modification review must verify "substantial change of circumstance."
Criteria for Change of Circumstances	Physical and emotional health needs; educational needs; day care costs or costs relating to child's age; change in custody status.
Frequency of Reviews	Every three years or less if there is a significant change of circumstance.
Criteria for Review	Order must be 3 years old or there must be a substantial change of circumstances.
Criteria for Adjustment	Physical and emotional health needs; educational needs; day care costs or costs relating to child's age; change in custody status.

NORTH DAKOTA

Interstate Procedures	Judicial process
Income Considered for Setting Support	All of the obligor's income excluding means-tested public assistance benefits.
Criteria for Rebuttal	Increased: need if support for more than 6 children sought; ability of obligor with monthly net income exceeding $10,000 or with increased assets; educational costs; medical needs; cost of child care. Reduced: ability to pay support due to expenses incurred to to visitation; ability of obligor to pay due to continued or fixed expense other than subsistence, work or daily living expenses; ability of obligor to pay due to medical needs.
Support Order for Prior Periods	Yes. IV-D will go back to date of assignment or birth (whichever later) for AFDC cases, or date of application for non-AFDC cases.
Jurisdiction Requirements	UIFSA, CEJ
Modification Procedures	If review determines modification is appropriate, parties have opportunity to stipulate. If no stipulation made, motion made to court and hearing may be held.
Criteria for Modification	15% change up or down; if current order provides for support payments in amount less than 85% or more than 115% of guideline amount.
Criteria for Change of Circumstances	Not specifically defined except: consideration of public assistance and availability of health insurance at reasonable cost.
Frequency of Reviews	3 years
Criteria for Review	Not reviewed if order or last review less than 35 months old; not conducted in Medicaid-only case if current order contains medical provisions or, in non-AFDC case, neither party requests review.
Criteria for Adjustment	15% change up or down; if current order provides for support payments in amount less than 85% or more than 115% of guideline amount.

OHIO

Interstate Procedures	Judicial and administrative via URESA petition.
Income Considered for Setting Support	All sources of income considered except for means tested income.
Criteria for Rebuttal	30 days from issuance of recommendations to dispute calculations.
Support Order for Prior Periods	Yes.
Jurisdiction Requirements	The order must be reviewed and adjusted in the initiating jurisdiction.
Modification Procedures	Complete within 180 days of request with an opportunity to challenge outcome with a hearing.
Criteria for Modification	10% variance in support award calculated using the guidelines.
Criteria for Change of Circumstances	30% change in income and resources for at least six months.
Frequency of Reviews	Every 36 months or sooner if 30% change has occurred.
Criteria for Review	36 months or 30% change in income or resources.
Criteria for Adjustment	10% variance

OKLAHOMA

Interstate Procedures	Handled same as local cases. Judicial or administrative process may be utilized to establish order for support.
Income Considered for Setting Support	Parents' gross income/assets; income can be imputed for either parent; actual cost of providing health insurance for child; support alimony or child support being paid by court order for other children not before the court.
Criteria for Rebuttal	Court can deviate if award inequitable, unreasonable or not in child's best interests, and specific finding of fact supporting such action must be made by court; when both parties represented by counsel, guidelines do not have to be followed.
Support Order for Prior Periods	Yes. 5 year limit for paternity establishment cases.
Jurisdiction Requirements	CEJ analysis under UIFSA.
Modification Procedures	AFDC cases reviewed on three year cycle. Non-AFDC reviewed upon written request if: review not conducted within last 30 months or completed within last 12 months, and significant change has occurred since last adjustment; non-custodial parent is located. If AFDC case, exception to 3 year cycle if non-custodial parent has employment related insurance, case is Medicaid and order does not include provision for medical support.
Criteria for Modification	Amount of award deviates 25% or more from existing order.
Criteria for Change of Circumstances	No clear definition other than not in compliance with child support guidelines.
Frequency of Reviews	3 year cycle
Criteria for Review	See Modification Procedures
Criteria for Adjustment	See Criteria for Modification

OREGON

Interstate Procedures	Oregon may use administrative process on any interstate request to establish a support order in accordance with UIFSA.
Income Considered for Setting Support	Evidence of other available resources to parent; reasonable necessities of parent; net income remaining after withholdings required by law or employment conditions; needs of other dependents; needs/hardships of child and/or parents; tax consequences; whether custodial parent remains at home to care for child; other spouse's income.
Criteria for Rebuttal	Special needs of child; cost of child's health insurance; child care costs; both parents' gross and net income/assets; second family involvement.
Support Order for Prior Periods	Yes; date of application or most recent referral or October 1, 1995, whichever is most recent and not previous to October 1, 1995.
Jurisdiction Requirements	Yes; current residence not required.
Modification Procedures	Administrative in accordance with UIFSA.
Criteria for Modification	After two years, change in circumstances not needed; if less than two years, requires proof of change in circumstances.
Criteria for Change of Circumstances	Material change continuing and unanticipated.
Frequency of Reviews	Every two years or upon request of either parent, or a guardian.
Criteria for Review	Every two years or upon request of either parent, or a guardian with proof of change in circumstances.
Criteria for Adjustment	Proven change of circumstances.

PENNSYLVANIA

Interstate Procedures	Judicial establishment procedure used.
Income Considered for Setting Support	Net income from sources including but not limited to: wages, salaries, fees, compensation in kind, commissions, property income, interest, rents, royalties, dividends, annuities, life insurance, endowment charge of indebtedness, partnership income, interest in estate or trust, military or railroad retirement benefits; social security and disability benefits; workers' compensation and unemployment compensation benefits.
Criteria for Rebuttal	Unusual needs or fixed obligations; other support obligations; other household income; ages of the children; assets of the parties; medical expenses not covered by insurance; standard of living of parties and their children; and other relevant and appropriate factors, including the best interests of the child(ren).
Support Order for Prior Periods	Date support request filed.
Jurisdiction Requirements	As long as this state remains the residence of obligor, obligee, or child for whose benefit the support order is issued, or until each individual party has filed written consent to modify order and allow state to assume continuing, exclusive jurisdiction.
Modification Procedures	Order must be registered in order to modify.
Criteria for Modification	Must show material and substantial change in circumstances for the mother, father or child. These changes must be reflected in the support guidelines.
Criteria for Change of Circumstances	Significant change in earnings or expenses for either party to the support action, or changes in needs for the child or children.
Frequency of Reviews	Orders are reviewed every 3 years.
Criteria for Review	Time or material change in circumstances.
Criteria for Adjustment	See Criteria for Modification

RHODE ISLAND

Interstate Procedures	Same as for in-state cases.
Income Considered for Setting Support	Obligor's income as presented by initiating jurisdiction (gross income).
Criteria for Rebuttal	None
Support Order for Prior Periods	No
Jurisdiction Requirements	Federal regulations are followed.
Modification Procedures	Increase or decrease in income, or increase in need
Criteria for Modification	Change of circumstances, time elapsed
Criteria for Change of Circumstances	Proof of need; proof of increased ability (income)
Frequency of Reviews	Every year upon request of either parent, or guardian. At least every three years for AFDC cases.
Criteria for Review	Timely request / age of order
Criteria for Adjustment	Proof justifying modification

SOUTH CAROLINA

Interstate Procedures	Administrative process used to extent possible; notices sent and agreement attempted. If not possible, judicial process employed; pleadings filed, defendant served, agreement attempted; if failed, judge will hear case.
Income Considered for Setting Support	Custodial parent's income; any income or source of compensation for non-custodial parent; assets of both parties; alimony
Criteria for Rebuttal	Standards of deviation from guidelines considered on a case-by-case basis
Support Order for Prior Periods	Yes; to date of genetic testing on paternity contested cases
Jurisdiction Requirements	CEJ analysis per UIFSA
Modification Procedures	Upon request in non-assistance cases and without request in AFDC cases, review for possible modification at least every three years. Uses current information, selection criteria, state statute requirements for child support and medical support obligations. Modification can be attempted if non-resident party submits to South Carolina jurisdiction. Orders may be adjusted based on changes of income of either party, if order works hardship on either party, if order is too low, if child is enrolled in high school past age of 18, or if medical insurance is very expensive. Proof of income/financial declarations required; pleadings completed by staff attorney.
Criteria for Modification	Change up or down of at least $25 or 20-25% of support amount.
Criteria for Change of Circumstances	No hard definition
Frequency of Reviews	Every three years
Criteria for Review	Order at least 3 years old; IV-D or medical support case; AFDC, MAO or IV-E Foster Care case; change in circumstances
Criteria for Adjustment	See above

SOUTH DAKOTA

Interstate Procedures	Same as local cases; non-custodial parent served with Notice of Support Debt and court order obtained utilizing income shares.
Income Considered for Setting Support	All sources of income, including disability
Criteria for Rebuttal	Support based on proportionate share of both parents' combined net incomes. It is presumed each parent is capable of earning minimum wage, except in cases of physical or mental disability.
Support Order for Prior Periods	Yes, limited to 6 years.
Jurisdiction Requirements	CEJ analysis per UIFSA
Modification Procedures	Either party may file a Petition for Modification of Child Support with the state office of child support enforcement. The circuit judge appoints a referee who schedules a hearing and recommends an order for support. If no objections, the court enters an order within 10 days. If there are objections, the court sets a hearing date and enters an order after the hearing.
Criteria for Modification	Change up or down of at least $25 per month and/or 20% unless medical insurance needs to be added, in which case there is no dollar/percentage requirement.
Criteria for Change of Circumstances	For orders entered after 7/1/89, a change of circumstances is required but not defined.
Frequency of Reviews	35 months
Criteria for Review	Locate not necessary; at least one of the parties resides in South Dakota in incoming request; order at least 35 months old.
Criteria for Adjustment	See Criteria for Modification

TENNESSEE

Interstate Procedures	Standard URESA petition required for establishment of support order.
Income Considered for Setting Support	Gross income/assets (award based on a flat percentage of net income as defined by state; gross income is needed to make this calculation)
Criteria for Rebuttal	Cost of health insurance for child; time spent with non-custodal parent; extraordinary medical or educational expenses; any other extraordinary expenses; foster care, extraordinary net income of obligor
Support Order for Prior Periods	Yes, to date of birth.
Jurisdiction Requirements	Standard URESA law
Modification Procedures	When there is a significant variance, as defined in guidelines, between guidelines and amount of support ordered.
Criteria for Modification	At least 15% or $15 per month
Criteria for Change of Circumstances	Drastic change in circumstances
Frequency of Reviews	Every 3 years
Criteria for Review	3 years since order filed or most recent petition to modify order; obligor's location is known; material change in circumstances permanent and involuntary
Criteria for Adjustment	See Criteria for Review

TEXAS

Interstate Procedures	Support order established by court based on Texas child support guidelines.
Income Considered for Setting Support	100% of all compensation paid or payable for personal services, however denominated. Statutory deductions for social security tax, federal withholding and income tax, union dues, cost of child's health insurance, and state income tax.
Criteria for Rebuttal	If application of guidelines would be unjust or inappropriate under the circumstances; outlined in detail in Texas Family Code Chapters 154.122 and 154.123.
Support Order for Prior Periods	Yes.
Jurisdiction Requirements	Texas must have or be able to assume CEJ.
Modification Procedures	Judicial modifications are used in interstate cases.
Criteria for Modification	If there is a change of circumstances, modification should be in accordance with guidelines.
Criteria for Change of Circumstances	There must be a change of circumstances of the child or person affected by the order that is material and substantial and has occurred since the date of the order. Modification must be in the best interest of the child.
Frequency of Reviews	Every 3 years in AFDC cases, or upon the request of either parent/guardian in non-AFDC cases.
Criteria for Review	Date of last review; whether locate information is available; whether request has been made.
Criteria for Adjustment	The order does not substantially conform with guidelines; 30% deviation from guidelines or support increases/decreases by minimum of $50 per month to meet modification; a substantial change in obligor income; substantial increase in the needs of the child.

UTAH

Interstate Procedures	Incoming cases the same as Utah cases; utilizes administrative process.
Income Considered for Setting Support	Compensation paid or payable for personal services, however denominated. Income from earned income sources is limited to the equivalent of one full-time job. However, if a parent consistently worked more than 40 hours per week prior to order, this income may be considered in calculating the guidelines.
Criteria for Rebuttal	Amount would be unjust, inappropriate, or not in the best interest of the child.
Support Order for Prior Periods	Yes (4 year limit for paternity establishment cases).
Jurisdiction Requirements	CEJ analysis per UIFSA
Modification Procedures	Review upon written request in non-AFDC cases and without a request in AFDC cases in a three year cycle; reviews of Utah court orders or Utah administrative orders can be requested. Court orders that require modification are referred to the Attorney General's office. Current information used to determine if award should be modified to bring order in compliance with state established guidelines.
Criteria for Modification	Change up or down of at least 25%; however, there are no requirements if modification is only to add a medical provision.
Criteria for Change of Circumstances	Utah law defines a 25% change as a change of circumstance and all other issues are dealt with on a case by case basis.
Frequency of Reviews	Every 3 years in non-AFDC cases; by the request of either parent, the guardian, or other state.
Criteria for Review	Automatically every 3 years in non-AFDC cases; by the request of either parent, the guardian, or other state.
Criteria for Adjustment	See above

VERMONT

Interstate Procedures	Judicial process
Income Considered for Setting Support	Income from any source; income from non-income producing assets over $10,000 other than primary residence and not more than $15,000 of a motor vehicle's value.
Criteria for Rebuttal	Ability to pay; deviation factors
Support Order for Prior Periods	Yes; establish support to date obligor would have known the child was his.
Jurisdiction Requirements	URESA
Modification Procedures	OCS reviews for modification non-public assistance orders at the request of either parent at any time; public assistance orders reviewed every three years. Modifications may be upwards or downwards, and medical support is included in review and in modification.
Criteria for Modification	Modification may be requested by either parent from the court upon the showing of a "real, substantial, and unanticipated change in circumstances."
Criteria for Change of Circumstances	A difference of more than 10% between current obligation and new obligation.
Frequency of Reviews	Every three years for public assistance cases; at the request of either parent at any time in non-public assistance cases.
Criteria for Review	Without request in public assistance, Medicaid-only, or IV-E Foster Care cases or with request in non-public assistance cases, and: 35 months since last order/review; non-custodial parent not in locate, not ANFC or SSI, incarcerated or institutionalized; case not in waiver status; current support obligation; at least 18 months before termination of order.
Criteria for Adjustment	Real, substantial or unanticipated change in circumstances, with 10% or more change in obligation amount

VIRGINIA

Interstate Procedures	Handled same as local cases. Virginia will enforce existing order; if no order exists and paternity not an issue, Virginia will establish administrative support order. If administrative establishment not possible, case will be taken to court for judicial establishment.
Income Considered for Setting Support	Combined monthly gross income of both parents from all sources. Spousal support included limited to support paid to pre-existing order/written agreement. Costs of health care and child care (due to employment of custodial parent) added to support obligation.
Criteria for Rebuttal	Administratively; multiple family cases; imputing income; also if an obligor is not satisfied with obligation, an appeal can be noted and referred to court; court may consider a number of other factors.
Support Order for Prior Periods	Yes
Jurisdiction Requirements	CEJ analysis per UIFSA
Modification Procedures	Either party in IV-D case, or an IV-D agency, may request in writing a review of obligation at any time. Whether requested or not, active AFDC, AFDC/FC, and Medicaid-only cases are reviewed every 36 months from date of most recent order; modifications may be for increases or decreases; reviews can be requested of support enforcement agencies or the court. If the child support is court ordered, and it is specified the order deviates from guidelines, enforcement agency petitions the court for a hearing. If it is not specified that the order deviates from guidelines, the enforcement agency asks the court to approve the Proposed Modified Order.
Criteria for Modification	An adjustment is made up or down if a material change in circumstance has occurred, defined as the difference between existing order and new obligation being at least 10% of existing amount, and change is at least $25 monthly.
Criteria for Change of Circumstances	Virginia law does not define change of circumstances.
Frequency of Reviews	Active AFDC, AFDC/FC, and Medicaid-only cases are reviewed every 36 months from date of most recent order; review at the request of either party of IV-D agency.
Criteria for Review	Review at any time at the written request of either party of IV-D agency.
Criteria for Adjustment	At the request of either party, or of another IV-D agency if there is at least 10% difference in amount of current obligation and new amount, and at least $25 change monthly

WASHINGTON

Interstate Procedures	Handled same as local cases; if order exists, Washington enforces existing order; if no order and paternity not an issue, administrative order for support entered.
Income Considered for Setting Support	Gross/net income/assets of both parents; non-recurring income, salary, wages, commissions, deferred compensation, overtime, contract-related benefits, dividends, interest, trust income, severance pay, annuities, capital gains, unemployment compensation, retirement benefits, spousal maintenance received, bonuses, disability benefits. Also, age and number of children, child care costs, special medical needs of child, cost of providing health insurance for child, second family involvement, long distance transportation expenses, and education expenses.
Criteria for Rebuttal	See RCW 26.19.075 "Standards of Deviation from the Standard Calculation"
Support Order for Prior Periods	Yes (5 year limit for paternity establishment cases)
Jurisdiction Requirements	CEJ analysis per UIFSA
Modification Procedures	Review upon written request in non-AFDC cases and without a request in AFDC cases in a three year cycle; review for child support or medical support, and for increases or decreases; when a child support order is inconsistent with Washington guidelines, the case is referred for modification action. All child support orders may be adjusted once every 24 months based upon income changes of either party without a showing of substantially changed circumstances, and also when: the order works severe economic hardship on either party, the child was age 0-11 when the order was set and is now 12-18 years old, the child is still in high school and has reached age 18; orders prior to June 7, 1984 may be modified to include health insurance. Mandated pleadings to initiate modification action are completed by DCS or attorney staff.
Criteria for Modification	Change up or down of at least $100 per month and 25%, total support change of at least $2,400 for life of the order; no dollar requirement if just adding medical support
Criteria for Change of Circumstances	No hard and fast definition of "substantial change of circumstances"
Frequency of Reviews	Every 3 years
Criteria for Review	Upon request in non-AFDC cases and without a request in AFDC, IV-E Foster Care or medical assistance only cases; IV-D or medical support case; order at least 35 months old; for Washington order, one party is a resident; for foreign order, both reside in state.
Criteria for Adjustment	See Criteria for Modification

WEST VIRGINIA

Interstate Procedures	URESA
Income Considered for Setting Support	Net income will be used until July 1, 1997, when Income Shares takes effect; use of gross income less payment of previously ordered child support, spousal support or separate maintenance; deduction for additional dependents may be allowed by court if obligor has other legal dependents.
Criteria for Rebuttal	Guidelines apply as rebuttable presumption; if court finds guidelines inappropriate, the court may disregard or adjust them to accommodate needs of the child or children or circumstances of either or both parents.
Support Order for Prior Periods	Yes
Jurisdiction Requirements	Under Full Faith and Credit, will attempt as long as one of the parties or the child continues to reside in West Virginia.
Modification Procedures	Investigation for modification conducted every three years, or at least once a year upon request of either party; both parties shall receive 30 days notice of review and the results of the review; if result of review is to seek modification of the order, a petition is filed and each party given 30 days notice of hearing.
Criteria for Modification	The child support order may be modified if there is a substantial and continuing change of circumstances.
Criteria for Change of Circumstances	If application of guidelines would result in a new order that is more than 15% different than the current order, the circumstances are considered to be a substantial and continuing change.
Frequency of Reviews	At least every three years, but no more than once a year.
Criteria for Review	Order is 36 months old; 15% deviation from child support; case lacks medical insurance, AFDC, medical assistance only, or IV-E foster care case without request.
Criteria for Adjustment	Order is 36 months old; 15% deviation from child support; case lacks medical insurance, AFDC, medical assistance only, or IV-E foster care case without request.

WISCONSIN

Interstate Procedures	Family Court Commissioners or judicial process, depending on the county.
Income Considered for Setting Support	All income except public benefits or child support received for a child.
Criteria for Rebuttal	Unfair to one or all parties
Support Order for Prior Periods	Birth of the child
Jurisdiction Requirements	UIFSA CEJ
Modification Procedures	UIFSA, s.769.303, s.769.611, s. 769.611 (b) (4)
Criteria for Modification	Conformance to guidelines
Criteria for Change of Circumstances	Earnings of obligor substantially increased or decreased; needs of a party or the child and substantially increased or decreased; children have extraordinary medical expenses not covered by insurance; a substantial change in child care expenses; passage of 33 months; receipt of AFDC by either parent; lack of conformance guidelines without reasons given; or by judicial decision.
Frequency of Reviews	Every 33 months, by request, or with a substantial change.
Criteria for Review	Request or order is 33 months old
Criteria for Adjustment	10% and at least 40% difference monthly

WYOMING

Interstate Procedures	Yes
Income Considered for Setting Support	Yes. Statutes require both parties income be used to determine support under income shares guidelines
Criteria for Rebuttal	Yes. Deviation Statutes
Support Order for Prior Periods	Child support is deemed effective at birth. Court limits arrearages to assigned support unless the non-custodial parent has been avoiding the establishment process or does not appear as ordered, or agrees otherwise.
Jurisdiction Requirements	CEJ
Modification Procedures	Yes
Criteria for Modification	20% change in the amount of current support or a substantial change of circumstances if child support is set in a property settlement agreement.
Criteria for Change of Circumstances	Any change considered "substantial" by the court.
Frequency of Reviews	Every three years by the IV-D program; private action can take place every six months.
Criteria for Review	34 months without review or modification.
Criteria for Adjustment	20% change in the amount of current support or a substantial change in circumstances.

APPENDIX II
STATE CHILD SUPPORT ENFORCEMENT AT A GLANCE

State	Program	# of Local Offices	UIFSA	URESA	RURESA
Alabama	State/county	67		✔	
Alaska	State	3	✔		
Arizona	State	8	✔		
Arkansas	State	25	✔		
California	County	58		✔	
Colorado	County/state	63	✔		
Connecticut	State	14		✔	
Delaware	State	3	✔		
District of Columbia	State/local	0	✔		
Florida	State	85		✔	
Georgia	State	54			
Hawaii	State	4		✔	
Idaho	State	8	✔		
Illinois	State	143	✔		
Indiana	State/county	N/A	✔		
Iowa	State	23		✔	
Kansas	State	31	✔		
Kentucky	State	19		✔	
Louisiana	State	12	✔		
Maine	State	12	✔		
Maryland	State	24	✔	✔	
Massachusetts	State	8	✔		
Michigan	State	N/A		✔	
Minnesota	State/county	83	✔		
Mississippi	State	84	✔		
Missouri	State	22		✔	
Montana	State	5	✔*		
Nebraska	State	11	✔		
Nevada	State/county	4		✔	
New Hampshire	State	12		✔	
New Jersey	State/county	21		✔	
New Mexico	State	7	✔		
New York	State/county	58		✔	
North Carolina	State	16	✔		
North Dakota	State/county	8	✔		
Ohio	County	88		✔	
Oklahoma	State	4	✔		
Oregon	State	N/A	✔		
Pennsylvania	State/county	67	✔		
Rhode Island	State	1		✔	
South Carolina	State	11	✔		
South Dakota	State	8	✔*		
Tennessee	State	31		✔	
Texas	State	68	✔		
Utah	State	6	✔		
Vermont	State	5			✔
Virginia	State	24	✔		
Washington	State	9	✔		
West Virginia	State	54		✔	
Wisconsin	County	72	✔		
Wyoming	State	9	✔		

* Did not adopt direct withholding by employers

How to save on attorney fees

How to save on attorney fees

Millions of Americans know they need legal protection, whether it's to get agreements in writing, protect themselves from lawsuits, or document business transactions. But too often these basic but important legal matters are neglected because of something else millions of Americans know: legal services are expensive.

They don't have to be. In response to the demand for affordable legal protection and services, there are now specialized clinics that process simple documents. Paralegals help people prepare legal claims on a freelance basis. People find they can handle their own legal affairs with do-it-yourself legal guides and kits. Indeed, this book is a part of this growing trend.

When are these alternatives to a lawyer appropriate? If you hire an attorney, how can you make sure you're getting good advice for a reasonable fee? Most importantly, do you know how to lower your legal expenses?

When there is no alternative

Make no mistake: serious legal matters require a lawyer. The tips in this book can help you reduce your legal fees, but there is no alternative to good professional legal services in certain circumstances:

- when you are charged with a felony, you are a repeat offender, or jail is possible

- when a substantial amount of money or property is at stake in a lawsuit

- when you are a party in an adversarial divorce or custody case

- when you are an alien facing deportation

- when you are the plaintiff in a personal injury suit that involves large sums of money

- when you're involved in very important transactions

Are you sure you want to take it to court?

Consider the following questions before you pursue legal action:

What are your financial resources?

Money buys experienced attorneys, and experience wins over first-year lawyers and public defenders. Even with a strong case, you may save money by not going to court. Yes, people win millions in court. But for every big winner there are ten plaintiffs who either lose or win so little that litigation wasn't worth their effort.

Do you have the time and energy for a trial?

Courts are overbooked, and by the time your case is heard your initial zeal may have grown cold. If you can, make a reasonable settlement out of court. On personal matters, like a divorce or custody case, consider the emotional toll on all parties. Any legal case will affect you in some way. You will need time away from work. A newsworthy case may bring press coverage. Your loved ones, too, may face publicity. There is usually good reason to settle most cases quickly, quietly, and economically.

How can you settle disputes without litigation?

Consider *mediation*. In mediation, each party pays half the mediator's fee and, together, they attempt to work out a compromise informally. *Binding arbitration* is another alternative. For a small fee, a trained specialist serves as judge, hears both sides, and hands down a ruling that both parties have agreed to accept.

So you need an attorney

Having done your best to avoid litigation, if you still find yourself headed for court, you will need an attorney. To get the right attorney at a reasonable cost, be guided by these four questions:

What type of case is it?

You don't seek a foot doctor for a toothache. Find an attorney experienced in your type of legal problem. If you can get recommendations from clients who have recently won similar cases, do so.

Where will the trial be held?

You want a lawyer familiar with that court system and one who knows the court personnel and the local protocol—which can vary from one locality to another.

Should you hire a large or small firm?

Hiring a senior partner at a large and prestigious law firm sounds reassuring, but chances are the actual work will be handled by associates—at high rates. Small firms may give your case more attention but, with fewer resources, take longer to get the work done.

What can you afford?

Hire an attorney you can afford, of course, but know what a fee quote includes. High fees may reflect a firm's luxurious offices, high-paid staff and unmonitored expenses, while low estimates may mean "unexpected" costs later. Ask for a written estimate of all costs and anticipated expenses.

How to find a good lawyer

Whether you need an attorney quickly or you're simply open to future possibilities, here are seven nontraditional methods for finding your lawyer:

1) **Word of mouth**: Successful lawyers develop reputations. Your friends, business associates and other professionals are potential referral sources. But beware of hiring a friend. Keep the client-attorney relationship strictly business.

2) **Directories**: The Yellow Pages and the Martin-Hubbell Lawyer Directory (in your local library) can help you locate a lawyer with the right education, background and expertise for your case.

3) **Databases**: A paralegal should be able to run a quick computer search of local attorneys for you using the Westlaw or Lexis database.

4) **State bar associations**: Bar associations are listed in phone books. Along with lawyer referrals, your bar association can direct you to low-cost legal clinics or specialists in your area.

5) **Law schools**: Did you know that a legal clinic run by a law school gives law students hands-on experience? This may fit your legal needs. A third-year law student loaded with enthusiasm and a little experience might fill the bill quite inexpensively—or even for free.

6) **Advertisements**: Ads are a lawyer's business card. If a "TV attorney" seems to have a good track record with your kind of case, why not call? Just don't be swayed by the glamour of a high-profile attorney.

7) **Your own ad**: A small ad describing the qualifications and legal expertise you're seeking, placed in a local bar association journal, may get you just the lead you need.

How to hire and work with your attorney

No matter how you hear about an attorney, you must interview him or her in person. Call the office during business hours and ask to speak to the attorney directly. Then explain your case briefly and mention how you obtained the attorney's name. If the attorney sounds interested and knowledgeable, arrange for a visit.

The ten-point visit

1) Note the address. This is a good indication of the rates to expect.

2) Note the condition of the offices. File-laden desks and poorly maintained work space may indicate a poorly run firm.

3) Look for up-to-date computer equipment and an adequate complement of support personnel.

4) Note the appearance of the attorney. How will he or she impress a judge or jury?

5) Is the attorney attentive? Does the attorney take notes, ask questions, follow up on points you've mentioned?

6)   Ask what schools he or she has graduated from, and feel free to check credentials with the state bar association.

7)   Does the attorney have a good track record with your type of case?

8)   Does he or she explain legal terms to you in plain English?

9)   Are the firm's costs reasonable?

10) Will the attorney provide references?

Hiring the attorney

Having chosen your attorney, make sure all the terms are agreeable. Send letters to any other attorneys you have interviewed, thanking them for their time and interest in your case and explaining that you have retained another attorney's services.

Request a letter from your new attorney outlining your retainer agreement. The letter should list all fees you will be responsible for as well as the billing arrangement. Did you arrange to pay in installments? This should be noted in your retainer agreement.

Controlling legal costs

Legal fees and expenses can get out of control easily, but the client who is willing to put in the effort can keep legal costs manageable. Work out a budget with your attorney. Create a timeline for your case. Estimate the costs involved in each step.

Legal fees can be straightforward. Some lawyers charge a fixed rate for a specific project. Others charge contingency fees (they collect a percentage of your recovery, usually 35-50 percent if you win and nothing if you lose). But most attorneys prefer to bill by the hour. Expenses can run the gamut, with one hourly charge for taking depositions and another for making copies.

Have your attorney give you a list of charges for services rendered and an itemized monthly bill. The bill should explain the service performed, who performed the work, when the service was provided, how long it took, and how the service benefits your case.

Ample opportunity abounds in legal billing for dishonesty and greed. There is also plenty of opportunity for knowledgeable clients to cut their bills significantly if they know what to look for. Asking the right questions and setting limits on fees is smart and can save you a bundle. Don't be afraid to question legal bills. It's your case and your money!

When the bill arrives

- **Retainer fees**: You should already have a written retainer agreement. Ideally, the retainer fee applies toward case costs, and your agreement puts that in writing. Protect yourself by escrowing the retainer fee until the case has been handled to your satisfaction.

- **Office visit charges**: Track your case and all documents, correspondence, and bills. Diary all dates, deadlines and questions you want to ask your attorney during your next office visit. This keeps expensive office visits focused and productive, with more accomplished in less time. If your attorney charges less for phone consultations than office visits, reserve visits for those tasks that must be done in person.

- **Phone bills**: This is where itemized bills are essential. Who made the call, who was spoken to, what was discussed, when was the call made, and how long did it last? Question any charges that seem unnecessary or excessive (over 60 minutes).

- **Administrative costs**: Your case may involve hundreds, if not thousands, of documents: motions, affidavits, depositions, interrogatories, bills, memoranda, and letters. Are they all necessary? Understand your attorney's case strategy before paying for an endless stream of costly documents.

- **Associate and paralegal fees**: Note in your retainer agreement which staff people will have access to your file. Then you'll have an informed and efficient staff working on your case, and you'll recognize their names on your bill. Of course, your attorney should handle the important part of your case, but less costly paralegals or associates may handle routine matters more economically. Note: Some firms expect their associates to meet a quota of billable hours, although the time spent is not always warranted. Review your bill. Does the time spent make sense for the document in question? Are several staff involved in matters that should be handled by one person? Don't be afraid to ask questions. And withhold payment until you have satisfactory answers.

- **Court stenographer fees**: Depositions and court hearings require costly transcripts and stenographers. This means added expenses. Keep an eye on these costs.

- **Copying charges**: Your retainer fee should limit the number of copies made of your complete file. This is in your legal interest, because multiple files mean multiple chances others may access your confidential information. It is also in your financial interest, because copying costs can be astronomical.

- **Fax costs**: As with the phone and copier, the fax can easily run up costs. Set a limit.

- **Postage charges**: Be aware of how much it costs to send a legal document overnight, or a registered letter. Offer to pick up or deliver expensive items when it makes sense.

- **Filing fees**: Make it clear to your attorney that you want to minimize the number of court filings in your case. Watch your bill and question any filing that seems unnecessary.

- **Document production fee**: Turning over documents to your opponent is mandatory and expensive. If you're faced with reproducing boxes of documents, consider having the job done by a commercial firm rather than your attorney's office.

- **Research and investigations**: Pay only for photographs that can be used in court. Can you hire a photographer at a lower rate than what your attorney charges? Reserve that right in your retainer agreement. Database research can also be extensive and expensive; if your attorney uses Westlaw or Nexis, set limits on the research you will pay for.

- **Expert witnesses**: Question your attorney if you are expected to pay for more than a reasonable number of expert witnesses. Limit the number to what is essential to your case.

- **Technology costs**: Avoid videos, tape recordings, and graphics if you can use old-fashioned diagrams to illustrate your case.

- **Travel expenses**: Travel expenses for those connected to your case can be quite costly unless you set a maximum budget. Check all travel-related items on your bill, and make sure they are appropriate. Always question why the travel is necessary before you agree to pay for it.

- **Appeals costs**: Losing a case often means an appeal, but weigh the costs involved before you make that decision. If money is at stake, do a cost-benefit analysis to see if an appeal is financially justified.

- **Monetary damages**: Your attorney should be able to help you estimate the total damages you will have to pay if you lose a civil case. Always consider settling out of court rather than proceeding to trial when the trial costs will be high.

- **Surprise costs**: Surprise costs are so routine they're predictable. The judge may impose unexpected court orders on one or both sides, or the opposition will file an unexpected motion that increases your legal costs. Budget a few thousand dollars over what you estimate your case will cost. It usually is needed.

- **Padded expenses**: Assume your costs and expenses are legitimate. But some firms do inflate expenses—office supplies, database searches, copying, postage, phone bills—to bolster their bottom line. Request copies of bills your law firm receives from support services. If you are not the only client represented on a bill, determine those charges related to your case.

Keeping it legal without a lawyer

The best way to save legal costs is to avoid legal problems. There are hundreds of ways to decrease your chances of lawsuits and other nasty legal encounters. Most simply involve a little common sense. You can also use your own initiative to find and use the variety of self-help legal aid available to consumers.

11 situations in which you may not need a lawyer

1) **No-fault divorce**: Married couples with no children, minimal property, and no demands for alimony can take advantage of divorce mediation services. A lawyer should review your divorce agreement before you sign it, but you will have saved a fortune in attorney fees. A marital or family counselor may save a seemingly doomed marriage, or help both parties move beyond anger to a calm settlement. Either way, counseling can save you money.

2) **Wills**: Do-it-yourself wills and living trusts are ideal for people with estates of less than $600,000. Even if an attorney reviews your final documents, a will kit allows you to read the documents, ponder your bequests, fill out sample forms, and discuss your wishes with your family at your leisure, without a lawyer's meter running.

3) **Incorporating**: Incorporating a small business can be done by any business owner. Your state government office provides the forms and instructions necessary. A visit to your state office will probably be

necessary to perform a business name check. A fee of $100-$200 is usually charged for processing your Articles of Incorporation. The rest is paperwork: filling out forms correctly; holding regular, official meetings; and maintaining accurate records.

4) **Routine business transactions**: Copyrights, for example, can be applied for by asking the U.S. Copyright Office for the appropriate forms and brochures. The same is true of the U.S. Patent and Trademark Office. If your business does a great deal of document preparation and research, hire a certified paralegal rather than paying an attorney's rates. Consider mediation or binding arbitration rather than going to court for a business dispute. Hire a human resources/benefits administrator to head off disputes concerning discrimination or other employee charges.

5) **Repairing bad credit**: When money matters get out of hand, attorneys and bankruptcy should not be your first solution. Contact a credit counseling organization that will help you work out manageable payment plans so that everyone wins. It can also help you learn to manage your money better. A good company to start with is the Consumer Credit Counseling Service, 1-800-388-2227.

6) **Small Claims Court**: For legal grievances amounting to a few thousand dollars in damages, represent yourself in Small Claims Court. There is a small filing fee, forms to fill out, and several court visits necessary. If you can collect evidence, state your case in a clear and logical presentation, and come across as neat, respectful and sincere, you can succeed in Small Claims Court.

7) **Traffic Court**: Like Small Claims Court, Traffic Court may show more compassion to a defendant appearing without an attorney. If you are ticketed for a minor offense and want to take it to court, you will be asked to plead guilty or not guilty. If you plead guilty, you can ask for leniency in sentencing by presenting mitigating circumstances. Bring any witnesses who can support your story, and remember that presentation (some would call it acting ability) is as important as fact.

8) **Residential zoning petition**: If a homeowner wants to open a home business, build an addition, or make other changes that may affect his or her neighborhood, town approval is required. But you don't need a lawyer to fill out a zoning variance application, turn it in, and present your story at a public hearing. Getting local support before the hearing is the best way to assure a positive vote; contact as many neighbors as possible to reassure them that your plans won't adversely affect them or the neighborhood.

9) **Government benefit applications**: Applying for veterans' or unemployment benefits may be daunting, but the process doesn't require legal help. Apply for either immediately upon becoming eligible. Note: If your former employer contests your application for unemployment benefits and you have to defend yourself at a hearing, you may want to consider hiring an attorney.

10) **Receiving government files**: The Freedom of Information Act gives every American the right to receive copies of government information about him or her. Write a letter to the appropriate state or federal agency, noting the precise information you want. List each document in a separate paragraph. Mention the Freedom of Information Act, and state that you will pay any expenses. Close with your signature and the address the documents should be sent to. An approved request may take six months to arrive. If it is refused on the grounds that the information is classified or violates another's privacy, send a letter of appeal explaining why the released information would not endanger anyone. Enlist the support of your local state or federal representative, if possible, to smooth the approval process.

11) **Citizenship**: Arriving in the United States to work and become a citizen is a process tangled in bureaucratic red tape, but it requires more perseverance than legal assistance. Immigrants can learn how to obtain a "Green Card," under what circumstances they can work, and what the requirements of citizenship are by contacting the Immigration Services or reading a good self-help book.

Save more; it's E-Z

When it comes to saving attorneys' fees, Made E-Z Products is the consumer's best friend. America's largest publisher of self-help legal products offers legally valid forms for virtually every situation. E-Z Legal Kits and the Made E-Z Guides which cover legal topics include all necessary forms and a simple-to-follow manual of instructions or a layman's book. Made E-Z Books are a library of forms and documents for everyday business and personal needs. Made E-Z Software provides those same forms on disk and CD for customized documents at the touch of the keyboard.

You can add to your legal savvy and your ability to protect yourself, your loved ones, your business and your property with a range of self-help legal titles available through Made E-Z Products.

Whatever you need to know, we've made it E-Z!

Informative text and forms you can fill out on-screen.* From personal to business, legal to leisure—we've made it E-Z!

Get Out Of Debt

Credit Repair

Vital Records

Living Wills
Includes Power of Attorney for Healthcare

Asset Protection

Buying/Selling Your Home

PERSONAL & FAMILY

For all your family's needs, we have titles that will help keep you organized and guide you through most every aspect of your personal life.

BUSINESS

Whether you're starting from scratch with a home business or you just want to keep your corporate records in shape, we've got the programs for you.

Incorporation

Corporate Records

Accounting

Your Profitable Home Business

Selling on the Web

Selling on the Web

* Not all topics include forms   ss 2001.r1

MADE E·Z® LIBRARY

MADE E-Z GUIDES

Each comprehensive guide contains all the information you need to learn about one of dozens of topics, plus sample forms (if applicable).

Most guides also include an appendix of valuable resources, a handy glossary, and the valuable 14-page supplement "How to Save on Attorney Fees."

Advertising Your Business Made E-Z
Learn the secrets and use the tools of the professionals.

Asset Protection Made E-Z
Shelter your property from financial disaster.

Bankruptcy Made E-Z
Take the confusion out of filing bankruptcy

Business Startups
Plan and start any home-based or small business.

Buying/Selling a Business Made E-Z
Position your business and structure the deal for quick results.

Buying/Selling Your Home Made E-Z
Buy or sell your home for the right price—right now.

Collecting Unpaid Bill Made E-Z
Get paid—and faster—every time.

Credit Repair Made E-Z
All the tools to put you back on track.

Divorce Made E-Z
Learn to proceed on your own, without a lawyer.

E-Commerce Made E-Z (Selling On The Web)
Welath-building, web-building strategies for any size business.

Employment Law Made E-Z
A handy reference for employers and employees.

Financing Your Business Made E-Z
Negotiate the best financing and grow your business.

Fund Raising Made E-Z
Magnetize big donations with simple ideas.

Get Out of Debt Made E-Z
Learn how to become debt-free.

Incorporation Made E-Z
Information you need to incorporate your company.

Last Will & Testament Made E-Z
Write a will the right way—the E-Z way.

Limited Liability Companies Made E-Z
Learn all about the hottest new business entity.

Living Trusts Made E-Z
Trust us to help you provide for your loved ones.

Living Wills Made E-Z
Take steps now to insure Death With Dignity.

Marketing Your Small Business Made E-Z
Proven marketing strategies for business success.

Money For College Made E-Z
Finance your college education—without the debt!

Multi-level Marketing Made E-Z
Turn your own product or service into an MLM empire.

Mutual Fund Investing Made E-Z
Build a secure future with fast-growth mutual funds.

Offshore Investing Made E-Z
Transfer your wealth offshore for financial privacy.

Partnerships Made E-Z
Avoid double taxation.

Profitable Mail Order Made E-Z
Turn virtually any product into a profitable mail order item.

Shoestring Investing Made E-Z
Amass more wealth with investments through strategic investing.

Stock Market Investing Made E-Z
Pick the best stocks and manage your own portfolio.

Solving Business Problems Made E-Z
Identify and solve business problems with proven strategies.

Solving IRS Problems Made E-Z
Settle with the IRS for pennies on the dollar.

Successful Resumes Made E-Z
Exploit your strengths, gain confidence, secure that dream job.

Winning Business Plans Made E-Z
Attract more capital—faster.

KITS

Each kit includes a clear, concise instruction manual to help you understand your rights and obligations, plus all the information and sample forms you need.

For the busy do-it-yourselfer, it's quick, affordable, and it's E-Z.

	ITEM#	QTY.	PRICE#	EXTENSION
Made E-Z Software				
Accounting Made E-Z	SW1207		$29.95	
Asset Protection Made E-Z	SW1157		$29.95	
Bankruptcy Made E-Z	SW1154		$29.95	
Business Startups Made E-Z	SW1192		$29.95	
Buying/Selling Your Home Made E-Z	SW1213		$29.95	
Corporate Records Made E-Z	SW1159		$29.95	
Credit Repair Made E-Z	SW1153		$29.95	
Divorce Made E-Z	SW1182		$29.95	
Everyday Law Made E-Z	SW1185		$29.95	
Everyday Legal Forms & Agreements	SW1186		$29.95	
Incorporation Made E-Z	SW1176		$29.95	
Last Wills Made E-Z	SW1177		$29.95	
Living Trusts Made E-Z	SW1178		$29.95	
Offshore Investing Made E-Z	SW1218		$29.95	
Your Profitable Home Business	SW1204		$29.95	
Made E-Z Guides				
Bankruptcy Made E-Z	G300		$17.95	
Incorporation Made E-Z	G301		$17.95	
Divorce Made E-Z	G302		$17.95	
Credit Repair Made E-Z	G303		$17.95	
Living Trusts Made E-Z	G305		$17.95	
Living Wills Made E-Z	G306		$17.95	
Last Will & Testament Made E-Z	G307		$17.95	
Buying/Selling Your Home Made E-Z	G311		$17.95	
Employment Law Made E-Z	G312		$17.95	
Limited Liability Companies Made E-Z	G316		$17.95	
Partnerships Made E-Z	G318		$17.95	
Solving IRS Problems Made E-Z	G319		$17.95	
Asset Protection Made E-Z	G320		$17.95	
Buying/Selling A Business Made E-Z	G321		$17.95	
Financing Your Business Made E-Z	G322		$17.95	
Profitable Mail Order Made E-Z	G323		$17.95	
Selling On The Web Made E-Z	G324		$17.95	
Solving Business Problems Made E-Z	G326		$17.95	
Advertising Your Business	G327		$17.95	
Shoestring Investing Made E-Z	G330		$17.95	
Stock Market Investing Made E-Z	G331		$17.95	
Fund Raising Made E-Z	G332		$17.95	
Money For College Made E-Z	G334		$17.95	
Marketing Your Small Business	G335		$17.95	
Owning A No-Cash-Down Business	G336		$17.95	
Offshore Investing Made E-Z	G337		$17.95	
Multi-level Marketing Made E-Z	G338		$17.95	
Your Profitable Home Business Made E-Z	G341		$17.95	
Winning Business Plans Made E-Z	G342		$17.95	
Mutual Fund Investing Made E-Z	G343		$17.95	
Business Startups	G344		$17.95	
Successful Resumes	G346		$17.95	
Get Out Of Debt	G340		$17.95	
Made E-Z Books				
Personnel Forms Made E-Z	BK408		$29.95	
Corporate Records Made E-Z	BK410		$29.95	
Vital Records Made E-Z	BK412		$29.95	
Collecting Unpaid Bills Made E-Z	BK409		$29.95	
Everyday Law Made E-Z	BK411		$29.95	
Everyday Legal Forms & Agreements	BK407		$29.95	
Workplace HR Posters				
Forklift Safety	HRP100		$9.95	
Forklift Safety (laminated)	HRP100L		$14.95	
Workplace Policies	HRP100		$9.95	
Workplace Policies (laminated)	HRP200L		$14.95	
Ergonomics	HRP300		$9.95	
Ergonomics (laminated)	HRP300L		$14.95	
Infection Control	HRP400		$9.95	
Infection Control (laminated)	HRP400L		$14.95	
Workplace Safety	HRP500		$9.95	
Workplace Safety (laminated)	HRP500L		$14.95	
First Aid	HRP600		$9.95	
First Aid (laminated)	HRP600L		$14.95	
Diversity Awareness	HRP700		$9.95	
Diversity Awareness (laminated)	HRP700L		$14.95	
Hazardous Materials	HRP800		$9.95	
Hazardous Materials (laminated)	HRP800L		$14.95	
☆ Federal Labor Law	LP001		$11.99	
☆ State Specific Labor Law — see state listings at right.			$29.95	
Total Quantity				

Shipping & Handling $3.50 for first item, $1.50 for each additional item	
Florida Residents add 6% sales tax	
TOTAL OF ORDER	

☆ Required by Federal & State Laws

Prices are for a single item as of 01/01, and subject to change without notice.

Name _____

Company _____

Organization _____

_____

Address _____

City _____ State _____ Zip _____

Phone (____) _____

PAYMENT

☐ check enclosed, payable to Made E-Z Products, inc.

☐ charge my credit card: ☐ MasterCard ☐ VISA   EXP.DATE ☐☐☐☐

ACCOUNT NO. | | | | | | | | | | | | | | | |

Signature: _____
(required for credit card purchases)

❋ FOR FASTRER SERVICE ❋

Order by phone:	Order by fax:
(954) 480-8933	**(954) 480-8906**

☆ *State Specific Labor Law*

Avoid up to $10,000 in fines by posting the required State Labor Law Posters available from Made E-Z Products. Posters include all mandatory postings for esch state.

State	Item#	QTY		State	Item#	QTY		State	Item#	QTY
AL	83801			KY	83817			ND	83834	
AK	83802			LA	83818			OH	83835	
AZ	83803			ME	83819			OK	83836	
AR	83804			MD	83820			OR	83837	
CA	83805			MA	83821			PA	83838	
CO	83806			MI	83822			RI	83839	
CT	83807			MN	83823			SC	83840	
DE	83808			MS	83824			S. Dakota not available		
DC	83848			MO	83825			TN	83842	
FL	83809			MT	83826			TX	83843	
GA	83810			NE	83827			UT	83844	
HI	83811			NV	83828			VT	83845	
ID	83812			NH	83829			VA	83846	
IL	83813			NJ	83830			WA	83847	
IN	83814			NM	83831			WV	83849	
IO	83815			NY	83832			WI	83850	
KS	83816			NC	83833			WY	83851	
TOTAL				**TOTAL**				**TOTAL**		

Company Purchase Orders welcome with approved credit.

All orders ship UPS Ground unless otherwise specified.

00850a BK.OF

Index

A-M

N-W